Between The Books

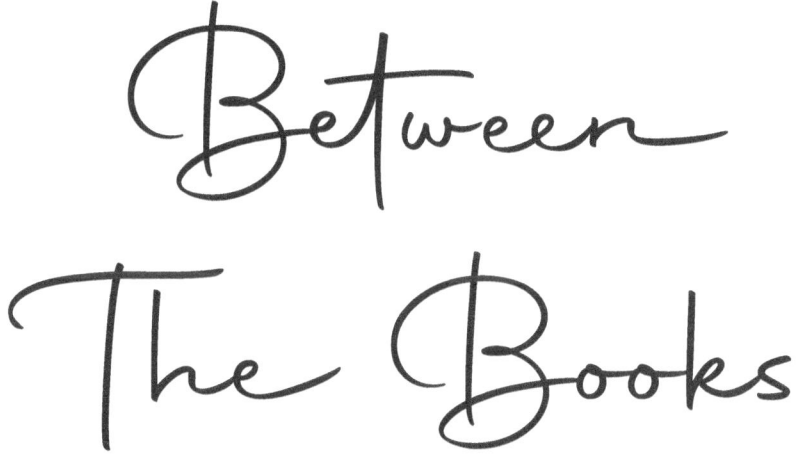

Between The Books

Collection of Poetry

2

1983–1990

Rosa M. Diaz

INKS & BINDINGS

Inks and Bindings
888-290-5218
www.inksandbindings.com
orders@inksandbindings.com

To my school friends
From Merced College,
1982-1984,
And CSU Stanislaus,
1894-1990,
Who acknowledged me
And made me feel special,
Wanted and respected.

INTRODUCTION

This is the continuation of INCIPIENT, Collection of Poetry I, 1977-1982.

With my high school graduation in 1982, a new phase of my life began. I had no plans of going to college. I thought that high school had given me all the education I needed to be a writer. I didn't realize that there are rules, steps, and techniques to follow and while learning about the basics, we also learn to write in our own style. I didn't realize college was a good place to acquire and develop ideas. Neither did I see that I needed social contact. I also needed to live through situations and emotions to write about at the moment or as in memories or visions. But, off to college I, went.

After the summer vacation, I enrolled at Merced Community College. All my childhood friends were scattered elsewhere. I was inhibited and alone, and frankly, I felt lonely too. I recognized some of my high school mates, but they pretended not to know me so I responded in the same manner.

The first few days were the most strenuous for me. I was like an abandoned kitten, scared, weak, and vulnerable, looking for my corner where I'd feel protected. A few days later, a young man with a particular dress style, kept coming my way trying to make conversation. Soon he became a good friend who kept me company in the afternoons, especially on Fridays when most everyone went home early. After that, I met another young man who insisted on making conversation when I wasn't in the mood to talk. But I am so glad he didn't give up on me because, with time, he became one of my best friends and he introduced me to many others who became very good friends.

I met so many people, each one in different circumstances and times. It was a special relationship with each one and they made me feel important with their attention and words. Amazing, in a few days everything started to change for the better. I was no longer alone. Now I looked forward to going to school to socialize with my friends and learn along the way.

My friends gave me their time and attention, their support and help, and their approval and encouragement. They also asked for my presence and my point of view on everything. Their problems and secrets fell on me. I listened, analyzed, and advised giving my frank and open opinion. I felt respected and safe among all of them. Amid everything, my self-esteem skyrocketed. I felt happy, confident, strong, defiant, and victorious.

We formed a big group of close friends with respect for the person, families, culture, and the responsibilities and rights of each person. I don't know if it was a thing of the times or something individual, but there was respect, discretion, and privacy. I am also happy to say that none of my friends ever said anything vulgar or rude and none of us were into drugs or even alcohol so the gatherings were always in a social and healthy manner.

These two years at MC were the best years of my life as a young adult. I never, before or after, had so many friends and the friendships were, never again, as strong and intimate as when I was 19-21 years old. I never again, spoke so freely and laughed so much or felt so positive and self-assured as in those days. For me, everything was good until the last days when we said goodbye and I transferred to the university.

In 1984 I transferred to CSU Stanislaus along with some other friends, but, although we were best of friends in one school, they, later, had other commitments, other goals, other people, and schedules and I was put in the category of acquaintances. I felt there was no time or interest to hear from me again and I move to the side. I thought that the alliance and camaraderie we had before would last and the closeness would not change, but at the university, there was no continuation or repetition.

MC brought me so many friends and high self-esteem, but CSU Stanislaus brought me down to a crude reality and back to my old insecure self. Being at the university and in the dorms, I was, once again, like a scared cat who wanted to keep in its corner, even if that corner was out in the open and in public. I didn't see it back then but the influence of an unhealthy relationship made things worse for me. But I loved that man and I was under the impression that he loved me too because he said it often.

It took me some time to meet more schoolmates, however, this time, I did not make as many friends and were never as close as in the previous school. Now the friendships were few, the gatherings were sporadic and the problems were more serious but less confiding.

MC and CSU Stanislaus brought me so many new things, including incidents, emotions, perspectives, knowledge, and understanding of myself and others. I started writing about my feelings and views outwards. I began to write down what was around me. I started writing about myself with a new point of view. Some professors at CSU Stanislaus saw my potential and directed me to creative writing classes where my love for writing was reinforced.

I graduated from the university in 1990 with the uncertainty of, now what? With the diploma at hand, a new phase of my life began. I hung the diploma on the wall along with my photo with the cap and gown to remind me of what I wanted to be and what I have lived through.

On the Contents page, I added an E to the poems that were originally written in English and an S to those originally in Spanish.

CONTENTS

REVERENCE

My reverence
Is to the Almighty Lord,
Who gave us a light
For our spirit,
Who makes us unique
In every meaning.

I am thankful
I am me
For I see
The beauty,
The magnificence
And the miracle
Of life
In ordinary little things.

A Prayer

Look after me
During the night,
Look after me
During the day,
You are
My only guide,
Without you
I am lost.
Make me good
To deserve
Your attention,
Save me
From the abyss,
Don't let me fall,
To the ground
Or onto temptation.

Look after
My awakening,
Look after
My dreams
That are beyond
My control,
Look after me
In my nightmares
Led by unwanted
Hands.
Don't let me
Be afflicted
By what
Has no way out
Or solution.

If I fail
And fall in sin,
Forgive me, Lord,
It was not intentional,
Just the hand
Of the devil on me.
Send an angel
To help me out
Through my fears
And guide me
Through my tragedies.

Look after
My thoughts
That stray away
In nothingness,
Remove
Any hindrance
And avert the evil
In my life,
Help me forget
The Mundane
And pay attention
To the spirit,
Help me find
Kindness in everyone
To help them
With no judgments.

You ought to know
I want to keep myself
Clean of sin
However, life is tough
When I look around
And cannot find you
Right here, by me.

Make me good,
Make me patient,
Have mercy on me,
Never leave me alone
Because I want
To touch heaven
With my own hands,
And experience paradise
With my senses.

Look after
My mortal soul
Today and the days
To come,
Look after
This tyrant world,
We all need you.

March 15, 1988

Soul And Light

The soul
And the light
Go hand in hand,
From childhood
To old age,
The soul reflects
Kindness,
The light
Illuminates
The personal
Happiness,
Both
Live on earth,
Both rise
To heaven
With its worth.

One,
Without the other,
Is nothing,
God sent a soul
To make us human,
The light
Arrived to us
To make us
Different.

The light
Is the essence
Of our personality,
The soul reflects
Our existence,
Both have
Their unique
Beauty,
Both are special
Sentimentally.
This, we know,
For what we do daily
And the promises
We accomplish.

The soul
And the light
Are strong
Like a tree,
The branches
Are the light,
The trunk
Is the soul.
The soul
And the light
Are like a flower,
The light
Is the aroma,
The beauty
Is the soul.
The light
And the soul
Are always united,
Like two friendly
Seagulls,
Like darkness
And the stars,
Like summer
And sunlight.

God
Takes the soul,
The light
Goes off by itself,
And of us —
Nothing is left.
Through time
The soul returns,
And the light shines
In another life,
Another being,
Since the reflection
Of this —
Never dies.

December 18, 1984

Man

Your hazel eyes
Reflect serenity
Illuminating
A heavenly peace,
Your face
Filled with kindness,
Gives smiles away
Wherever you go.

Your words,
Always bound
To God's words,
Bring hope
To everyone,
At every time.
Friend
Of the universe,
Your voice
Is a sweet chant
Brought
By the saints
And close to you
Everything is peaceful.

Your body
Is the image repeated
In thousands
Of ancestors
But at the same time,
You are special,
You are unique.

You are
The helpful hand,
Always ready
To help anyone
Because the Lord
Is with you.

Man,
Converted by Jesus
As a guide,
Has much to give
In your daily life,
The strength
Of your faith
Is reflected
In the actions
Humbly taken
Toward the neighbors
With no complaints.

May 23, 1984

The Cathedral

The cathedral
Was so beautiful,
Seemed so near
And yet so far,
Just a few steps away
As I walked by it.

I came to leave
My sins
In its enormous
Walls
And beautiful
Construction,
And I came
To be forgiven.
My tears cleaned
My conscience,
And the deep silence
Made an echo
That deafened me.

I felt a peaceful
Restlessness,
I forgot the world
Outside,
And I entered a world
Of transparency,
I had nothing to hide,
Everything
Was exposed.

I wished to stay there
Forevermore
But, suddenly,
I felt fear
To the rectitude
To my faults
And shame
To face them.

I went outside,
And the light
Blinded me,
I preferred to live
In a world
Of sinners, liars
And villains,
But knowing
That each action
May take me
To know the pure
And clean love
That the spirit needs
To rise above all.

October 30, 1983

Do Not Fear

When you feel sad,
Remember me,
I will be there
To cheer you up,
Do not feel bad,
There is nothing to fear.

Never feel lonely
Trust me,
I will always be
By your side,
Always near,
To help you
Solve your problems
That may appear.

Forget the pain
Of the past,
Live intensely
The happiness
Of today,
Because in the end,
That's all that lasts.
Do not imagine
Your future,
Or you may be
Disappointed
As what you are hoping
May not come true.

Don't fear,
Pay attention,
You're not alone,
Even if you
Don't see it,
God's Spirit
Is always near.

Live only
One day at a time,
And enjoy
The precious life.
God
Is your best guide
And the guardian angel
Is in your mind.

October 19, 1983

On My Knees

I get on my knees,
On the cold hard floor
By my bed,
I pray to God
For my health,
My well-being
And my mental strength.
I pray for my life,
I pray to ease the fears
That make me agonize.
Please, give me
A long peaceful
And healthy life.
—I am not ready
To die.

My long, serious
And complex
Imagination
Worsen my health.
I live in conflict
Of depression
And perpetual worries
That cause me
Faints, dizziness,
And episodes of silence.

Fears constantly
Disturb my mind
And well-being.
With devotion, I pray
For my health

And for my fears
To go away.
I sincerely offer
Everything I have
And with devotion,
I pray that God
Extends my life
To prove my worthiness.

I learned to pray
Each night
And be grateful
For what I have.
With each day
That passes by,
I know
I am more in debt
With God
And the angels
He sends
From up above.

August 5, 1985

L
O
V
E

Love
Is the strongest
Emotion,
That makes us thrive,
We strive
To earn it,
We work
To keep it.
True love
Never dies
But most forget
And never appreciate
The feeling they had.

Love
Has strong
Counterparts
And because of love,
We live sadly
Or happy,
Disappointed
Or dreaming,
It's a circle of life
And living.

To Love
And Be Loved

Loving
Fills the heart
With happiness
And hope
Just as we see
That face,
Just as we hear
One word
From those lips.

As we love,
We laugh,
We cry,
We struggle,
We suffer,
We experiment,
We live.
To love
Brings happiness,
We live
Off hope,
We dream,
We set goals,
We have faith
And barriers vanish.
The soul
Makes the effort
To improve the self.

We love
With the mind,
Body and soul,
Everything
Looks beautiful,
Everything
Looks divine,
We offer,
We gift away,
We give life itself
Without asking
For anything back,
The heart
Is satisfied
With each action
Done
For the one
We love.

When we are loved,
The world
Keeps its routine
And we wish
To escape
And pursue
Another life.
We wish
To be distant
From the happiness
Others feel
And don't understand
Why all the sighs
Or words
Are omitted.

When we are loved,
The heart fills up
With pride
And satisfaction
To boast
Of ourselves.
We become selfish,
Insensitive,
Indifferent,
At times,
We are ruthless
And cruel
With the one
Who loves us.
The heart
Has no dreams,
It has
No hopes
Or options,
It's all plain
And monochrome.

Sometimes,
When we are loved,
We can love back
With gratitude,
Courtesy,
Or compensation
But there is no
Honesty
Or contentment,
We live
A routine life
But acceptance
Is not
With happiness.

But when love
Is freely reciprocated,
The union
Can do everything
And life
Becomes one.

October 20, 1983

Our Creation

My sweetheart,
Love
Brought us together,
And as a reward
For that feeling,
God sent us a child.

What a joy,
What despair,
Will he be born
At nighttime
Or in the day?
Will he brag about
His self-image?
Will he be arrogant
Or humble
And friendly?
Will he be honest
Or a hypocritical liar?

Will he be like you
Or will he be like me?
Many questions,
Many expectations,
And many dreams
But I want him to have
Your eyes,
Your voice
And your demeanor.
He'll be like you.
I surely want this.

We all change
With time
And experiences.
But we'll be with him
Through everything.
Of us,
His parents,
He'll not be ashamed.
He'll know
That no one
Will be with him
And by him
Like us.

My sweet,
Beautiful child,
He'll give charity
With pleasure.
He'll be brave
And will defeat all
In his path
In pursuit of his goal
Because he deserves
And works for it.

My baby,
Child of my life,
Child of my dreams,
Child of my wishes,
Your father
Will be your partner
And I, your friend.
Of my worries
You'll be the owner.

I'll make you a prince,
I'll make you a king —
Never a beggar.
And I promise it
Like a sacred law.

Our creation,
Wonderful thing,
Heavenly creature,
Comes to fill
The emptiness
Of my heart
And home
With satisfaction.
There'll be toys,
Laughter and cries,
Joys and anger,
Covering the echoes
Of the most intimate
Corners.

Thank you, God,
For listening
To my prayers,
For giving me a child
Who'll be
Very much loved.

November 31, 1986

Sweethearts

Who's that boy,
Who, at a distance,
Often goes by,
Looks at me
And smiles so flirty?
Who is he?
I'm intrigued
But I don't dare
Move from my seat.
In the end,
He comes to me.

For a while,
He became
An acquaintance
With lots of smiles
And glances
And I pursued
A relationship
Or as friends.
He was fun
And interesting
When he was nice
And friendly,
When he wanted to,
He was sociable,
And happy,
When he didn't,
He was moody,
Indifferent,
And demanded his space.

Months of chasing him
Got me nowhere
And I came to the end
Of my patience.
The January frost
Let me see
How stupid I was.
It didn't matter much,
I gave up on him,
I took away the worth
I placed on him,
It was direct,
Loud and clear,
He'd not have a glance
Or a greeting.

It came easier
Than I thought,
To pass by him
And greet everyone,
Except him,
It was easy to pretend
He didn't exist
And give him the space
He wanted
But seeing the pain
In his face was hurtful.

Well, well,
What do we have here?
It didn't take long,
We switched places,
I became stern
And heartless
But there was a light touch
Or a smile

From his part
As we crossed each other
In the halls
Or the stairs
And he became
A familiar stranger.
Unwittingly,
A taste
Of his own medicine
Altered the outcome
Of destiny.
The stranger
Now pursued me
Smiling provocatively.

It was just a crush,
Something
I could live without,
A fleeting dream,
Nothing more,
But little by little
I gave in.

He had the lead
And the means,
In the newly found
Friendship,
The invitations
To get away
Never ceased
And we talked
About everything
And laughed
At nothing at all.

It became
A relationship
On a spring day
When he asks
If I want to be
His girlfriend.
I never thought
This day would come
But I welcomed it
Nonetheless.

His kisses
And caresses
Were of my delight
But the joy
To my senses
Was to hear him say
He loved me.

I was on cloud nine,
I earned his attention
And love
And it was better
To have him
Among all my friends.

June 11, 1984

Ironies

You wanted to be
My protector
But you're still a child
Looking for love
And protection.
You wished to be
My idol, my hero,
But you're the villain,
Selfish man,
Unable to see
Beyond yourself.

Your eyes of sin
Denounced me,
And I felt inferior.
Your suspicions
And accusations
Filled my mind
With remorse
Of this relationship
But this caused
Pleasure in you
And gave rise
To the brutal force.

You wanted me
As your lover,
But you're no one's friend.
You wanted to be
My confidant,
But you don't try
To understand.

You demanded
My honesty,
And you are
A fatal liar.
You demanded
My oath,
And time proved you
An actor.
You were
Hypocritically kind,
In the end,
You're a man
With no pride.

Poor man,
I feel sorry for you,
Insecure child,
Unwisely smart,
Wanted to succeed
And became
A great loser
When you saw
That I, this woman,
Is leaving you.

You killed my love
By strikes,
With your vain
Actions
And hollow words
And evil thinking.
I was a victim
Of your snubs,
And now
You are a victim
Of my indifference.

You were so proud,
Now humbly
You come to beg.
Yesterday
You were so arrogant,
And today,
You have no shame.

Look
How things are,
Yesterday,
I was so weak,
And at your service,
Today,
I am strong and brave.
Ironies of life,
When things
Are not meant to be,
Even if forced,
It never goes right.

As you lose me,
On your knees
You beg
For me to come back,
But I want
Nothing more
With you.
The ironies of life
Hurt more
When they turn
Against us
Without any hints
That would lead us
To suspect.

I don't judge,
It's what you learned,
Your cruelty
Will follow you
Like the shadows
Of your sins.
The consequences
Of your actions
Will be with you
Like the beat
Of your conscience.
If you don't change,
You'll destroy
Your existence.
Your conscience
Will forever
Give you the answer.
If you feel guilty,
You know deep inside
You've done wrong.
If you're happy,
It's because God
Has sent you peace.

I forget all evil,
In my heart
I found the answer
That keeps me content.
Today your pride
Is hurt,
You didn't believe
I would confront you
With so much
Inner strength.
But you see,
I've learned.

You'll hurt me
No more,
I will no longer hear
You scream,
Here, each one
Take its route.
Don't worry
About me.
I pray that God
To blesses you
And forgives you.
I am sure
That being apart
We'll do much better.

April 10, 1989

If You Ever

If you ever
Need a helping hand,
I will be there
Because I really care
And, for your life,
I want the best.

If, on any holiday,
You feel sad
And lonely,
Don't ever doubt it
You can count
On me,
To make you happy,
My dear friend.

If the cold
Of winter
Makes you yearn
For the warmth
Of a friend,
Remember me.
I will be there,
When you need
My help,
If you allow it,
I will be there,
Forever.

December 20, 1987

Promises
Of The Heart

I promise,
When you have
A problem,
When you're sad,
Don't fear,
Call me,
I will make you
Smile.

If you're depressed
Or if you're hurting,
Turn to the sky
And see the sun
That shines daily,
Open your eyes
And see
That nature
Brings hope
And life.

Don't doubt
What I say.
Before the tragedy
There is comfort.
Before the loss
There is advice
That I promise
To give
To calm
Your suffering.

I promise
To be there
In case
Of an emergency,
Or in case
Of loneliness.
When you feel
Like crying,
When you are sad,
I'll toss your pain
Onto the skies
To see it fly away
Like dust
In the air.

If you need
A friend,
If you need
A lover,
I'll be with you
In a moment
To give you
Affection
And share
My happiness.

When you're cold,
I'll share
My warmth,
I promise to respect
And be understanding
To your suffering
And pain.

I promise,
From my heart
To your heart,
To be with you
In good
And bad times,
As no one
Has been,
As no one
Will ever be.

Promises are,
But it's up to you
To make them
Come true.
When you need me,
If you call,
I will help.
But
If you don't tell me,
I won't know
What's afflicting
Your soul,
Mind, and heart.

October 17, 1988

First Kiss

A little before
My thirteenth year,
In a party
Half lighted,
A boy,
Much older,
Detected me,
Approached me,
And sat next to me.
He talked
And asked questions
But the music
Was too loud
So I smiled at him
As I couldn't hear.

Suddenly,
As I turned
To look at him,
He planted such a kiss
On my lips,
— It was direct.
I knew not
What to do
Or how to react.
I was a girl,
Innocent, inexperienced
To anything like this
But I closed my eyes
Automatically.
I was under his control
And charm.

It was a kiss
Divided in two
For a second of air
That he,
As leader
And teacher,
Took in between.
He wanted to probe
And teach me,
But my mouth
Was like a prison
With chains
And screws of steel.

His tenacious
And impatient lips
Dominated my senses,
It was a kiss
That lasted seconds,
But left me stunned
And asking for more,
However,
I made no attempt
To suggest anything
Because
My reputation
Was on the line.

I don't know why,
When we separated,
I felt shame,
For him, for me,
And whoever had seen.
I lowered my face,
Wishing he'd leave
But he took my hand

Between his hands,
Oh so gently,
And we remained so
For a few minutes,
Until it was time
To go.

He accompanied
The bunch of girls
To the house,
We all walked
Without worries,
Words and laughter
Filled the dark
And deserted streets.

I went to sleep
With a new
Perspective on life
And the sensation
Of his lips over mine
Still fresh in my mind.
I went to sleep
With sighs and smiles
That made me dream
All night.

A kiss
Of a few seconds
Was of great impact,
It awoke in me
Emotions and dreams,
Provocations,
And the words,
I love you.

Two months later,
For my First
Communion,
I should've confessed
All my sins,
But I kept
This one quiet,
It was a secret
Between me
And my conscience.

The first kiss
Was so private
That for many years
It stayed hidden
Like a buried treasure
In the subterranean
Chamber
Of my mind.
I know God knows
And understands
How things are
In love,
Even if not spoken,
Things are asked and given.

November 22, 1987

Doesn't Matter

Doesn't matter,
I tell you,
Repeating it
To myself
One thousand times.
Doesn't matter,
Don't worry,
I am fine,
I know destiny
Plays its tricks.

Though it hurts
And angers me,
I tell you,
It doesn't matter.
I tell you
It doesn't matter
And I curse you.
I wish
You'd feel guilty,
I wish
You'd feel remorse,
I wish
You'd feel sorry
For leaving me
Waiting
With not even
A phone call
To tell me
You won't show up.

I am your friend,
I like to listen
And help
But I am not a rag doll
That you can do
And undo
At your pleasure.
I am human,
I have feelings,
And here, I tell you
I am sorry,
But amid my anger
And pain
I curse you
And pity you too.

If I want to see you
Or not,
Any which way
I feel guilty
And end up sad.
Perhaps
I am selfish
And want things
My way,
When I don't get it,
It all seems wrong
And silly.

I've lost
Many friends
For being as I am,
And the ones
I still have
Don't appreciate me,
Either,

I demand too much
Or they expect
Too much from me.

When I cry
And free my soul,
Then I'll ask
To be forgiven,
But meanwhile,
With knots
In my throat
And heart
And anger
In my hands,
I tell you,
It doesn't matter.

I can wait,
I am just a friend
Who is a friend
To listen.
But for me —
Who listens to me
As I do with others?
Perhaps
I demand too much,
But in the crisis,
Who stops to think?

Doesn't matter.
Go on, have fun,
Fulfill your life,
I understand
The barriers
That life imposes.
But then,

When you need
A friend,
I might tell you,
I am sorry,
It doesn't matter to me.

Doesn't matter,
I can wait,
Doesn't matter,
I am fine.
Just remember,
He, who is not present,
May lose something.
If you don't understand
All that I have said,
Read and analyze
This again.

October 28, 1988

28

Temptation

Temptation
Seized my mind
And body,
As I set free
My inhibitions,
I feel fulfilled
But not satisfied.

I hungered
For your body,
I was thirsty
For your kisses,
My thoughts
And flesh
Said yes,
But my soul
Did not conceive
To be just a fling.

Many times
I kept my feelings
Very quiet
Out of fear
Of offending anyone.
Many times
I ignored my desires
Out of fear
Of being humiliated.

The cold of winter
Makes me tremble,
The stillness of the night

Makes me yearn
The warmth
Of another person,
My mischievousness
Burdens my mind,
My heart is on fire,
And my mind
Cannot rationalize.

Strange relationship
This is,
In the friendship
There is flirting
And seduction,
In the eyes
There is temptation
And in the touch
There is fire.

Wicked temptation,
Because of you
I am called audacious.
Now I see,
Winter is mates
With the internal agony,
Darkness is friends
With the evil temptation
And I am between all.
Without thinking more,
I give myself
To the passionate
Intrigue.

November 28, 1988

Lovers

Of our night
Of passion
Only memories are left
But I still feel
The sensation
Of your kisses,
The fragrance
Of your body
Still lingers on mine.

I wanted
To make you happy,
And you
Only wanted
To satisfy
Your temptations.
Among the caresses
And kisses
You forgot
About my feelings.

I wanted to fill you
With pleasure,
I wanted to satisfy
Your passion,
I wanted to find love,
But I only
Encountered sin.

Now I know
That true love
Is not
To be searched for.
No.
It likes to arrive
As a surprise
And secretly.

January 21, 1988

The Breakup

Years wasted,
Years given
To what turned out to be
A fleeting dream,
Years assuming
I was in a serious
Relationship,
But I was deceived
He never loved me.

The man I love,
The man who, daily,
Told me he loved me,
Set the idea
Of a wedding,
A home, children
And a forever together.
It was in the air
And timeline
I, too, wanted it
For the love I felt,
And to appease
Those that judge
And criminalize
With old rules
That no longer pertain.

I didn't see
The marriage proposal
Got farther away
When the word 'Soon'
Became 'One day,'

And then the excuses
Of 'Studies,
Job and family,'
Appeared in order
And his interests shifted
Right in front of my face.

His words of love
Blinded me,
His touch was soft,
His kisses were sweet
And his embrace
Was tender
But his company
Was dishonest
And his mind
Was deceptive.
His lying words
Covered the silence
And his hypocrisy
Concealed his emptiness.

His wandering eyes
Found new entertainment
Or she found him,
But she coaxed him
And I became
A nuisance in his path.
How painful it was,
It hurt my head
And my heart.
In a synchronized act,
I pushed away
The man I love,
He walked away
In a hurry

And she waited for him
With open arms
On her bed.

The man I love left.
The breakup
Hurt so much,
I fell to the floor
And cried
Until I fell asleep.
I felt as if death
Fell over me
From the intense pain,
The emptiness, the silence,
The loneliness
And the deceit
He left behind.

I was accustomed
To his caress,
And his flattery
And amid everything,
He was good company
When he was
In a good mood.
I felt lost,
My future alone
Was unconceivable
And I asked myself,
What am I going to do
Without him?

My depression
Turned into isolation
And an internal battle.
I missed his voice,

His laughter,
His hand and his presence
That filled my apartment.
I wanted to have back
The man I loved
But I didn't want
The deceiving man.

Days apart
Turned everything
Against me.
Gossip and blame
Ran free
And it became
A circle of grievances.
It's as if they were waiting
For the breakup
To talk and accuse
And make
Their conjectures.
The victim
Was turned into the villain
And the culprit came out
As the hero of the story.

I let myself
Be knocked down
By the words
Of insignificant people.
My self-doubt showed up
With many questions,
Criticism and complaints
That saddens me
And made me regret
What I lived.
Who'd want

To love me now?
I already gave myself away
To an undeserving man
Who never loved me.

The wounds of deceit
Opened up and bled
With the empty promises
Of his return,
His regrets
And the 'I love you'
That never ended.
My pain obstructed
My view
To the outside world.
Seemed like an eclipse
Covered the earth,
But no, it was
Just my eyes,
Teary and exhausted
That couldn't see.

I wanted it
To be night all-day
To cry endlessly
But the sun
Kept rising
Each morning
And I saw no choice
But to wake up
And rise up with it.
Time and the sun
Helped me get up,
Dust off
And carry on.

For a mind
Full of prejudices
And conventionalisms,
My actions
Were my sin
And my shame
And my secret life
That I protected so much
Came to light
When I announced
I carry a baby inside.

December 31, 1990

Perhaps

If I offended you,
I'm sorry,
It wasn't my intention
To say
Meaningless things.

I'd like to see you
And talk about the past,
Perhaps I boast,
But maybe this way
Our hearts
Could be linked
From now on.

You decide,
You choose,
I did my part,
But I tell you,
Don't throw away
These feelings
To the emptiness
Without consulting
With me first.

February 21, 1987

Bravery

In a culture
Where fathers
Have the utmost respect
And have the first
And the last word,
Where men,
As prospects or suitors,
Enter the house
Only until marriage,
And where
The rules at home
Are of obedience,
Respect and silence,
Are now contradicting
What we live
And learn in this country.
But being young,
Being a woman
And wanting to have fun
Don't add up
With the parents.

I wanted to keep
My beau a secret
And in public
We'd be friends,
He'd keep his distance
And I'd watch my words
To prevent more rules
From vigilant eyes
And loose tongues.

How I wish
We were more modern
And able to go out
And talk with anyone
Free of guilt
And limited time.
I wish the suitors
Were able to visit
To know each other better,
But here, customs
Are fundamental.

But, what do I see?
My heart skips a beat,
My beau arrives,
With that disposition
Of bravery, audacity
And determination
But smiles graciously
And respectfully
Introduces himself
To my father.

They talk about me
As if I was away,
They dispute my future
As they discuss
Rules and my upbringing
Morality and honor.
One raised me
And demands respect,
The other one
Sees me as a woman
And asks for permission
To know me better.
It seems this is the moment

Where two stages
Of my life
Greet and say goodbye.

The beau
Wants to know me
With no interference
But there's static
In this conference.
My father
Gives a stern look
From the corner
Of his eye,
He listens
To the young man
As he smokes
But, at the same time,
Familiar voices
With severe tone
Meddle in
With their complaints
That echoed
Against me.

The beau asks
Expecting an answer,
'I want to take her out
With no problems.
Do we have
Your permission?'
My father
Sits in his chair
And takes a sip of coffee
And the question
Remains in the air.

I feared
An impulsive reaction
As he became restless,
Because, how dare
A simple man
Disrupt the order
Of the home
And trouble the ruler
In his domain?

The comments go on,
Everyone speaks
At the same time,
The many intruders
In the conversation,
With killer eyes
And with their tone
Of voice,
Want to manipulate
The outcome.
The beau's petition
Lays a big
And serious offer
To bring his parents
And prove
He's a good-hearted man.

Wow, this man
Is impressive.
Standing up to the man,
His resilience
On this situation
And his tenacity
To get time with me
Are the biggest
Proof of love

He can give me.
He's doing all this
For me,
I sigh,
I see how great he is.
My father looks up
And contemplates
The situation.
'Alright bring your parents
So I can give you
My answer.'

The clock
Must be broken,
Time stays still,
The second hand
Moves so slow
But twenty-four
Hours pass,
Twenty-four hours
Of anxiety,
Twenty-four hours
Of uncertainty
And expectations
But my beau is back
As part
Of the commitment.

They repeat
The son's characteristics
And best intentions.
Then, the question
For my father
Comes up again,
'I want to take her out
With no problems.

Do we have
Your permission?'
Am I allowed to come
Into your house?'

There are
No more excuses
Or postponements
To his answer,
Silence is excruciating
But in his sad eyes
I see he's aware the culture
And his control
Are being questioned
And challenged.

Words come out
Of his mouth
Mixed with smoke,
'All right,
But you two will respect
This house
And my rules,
And you two behave,
I want no nonsense.'

I translated and decoded
What he said
And meant to say.
There are times
When embarrassment
And lack of words
Are a strong pretext
To avoid the topic
And not teach
What we've learned.

It's assumed
Others understand
On what is expected
Of them
It's assumed
They know the facts
Of life
And will maintain
Composure
To have honor and respect
To avoid
A rude awakening.

There are things said
And accepted in code
Even if they're never
Cleared or explained.
As for me,
I've learned on my own
What no one ever mentions.

August 20, 1984

Innocence

The chattering
Turns serious,
The voices
Turn into whispers,
I look at his lips
And start wondering,
The touch of his fingers
On my hand
Feel like fire.
The eyes of the man
I am attracted to,
Signal me to follow him,
Without hesitation,
I do as I am directed.

I walk tripping
On my own feet,
The anticipation
And the excitement
Create new emotions
Of anxiety, provocation,
Desires and temptation.
Imagination runs free
On what could be a kiss.

A friendly look
And a flirty smile
Appear on his face
And I fall
On the enchantment
Of the beast.
As a courteous man,

He opens the car door
And invites me in.

The streetlight
Penetrates softly
Through the front window
And illuminates
Parts of his face.
The sight
Of the empty
And dark area
Bring chills to my spine
As I focus
On the cool of the night.

His lips are soft,
His kissing is slow
His touch is tender,
His hands caress me,
He kisses me
Once or twice on the lips,
He touches and probes
Here and there
And buries his face
In the locks of my hair.

My lips on his
Also participate
But with reservations,
I hold back,
Don't know what to do.
Everything is new
And the experience
Is confusing.
Am I supposed
To do something?

What would
He think of me
If I make a move?
His lips and mine
Encounter each other
But at a different rhythm.
He undresses me
In an instant,
I want to say No
But I never hear me
Mutter anything.

I feel fragile
In his hands
And innocence is lost
At dusk
In early spring
While the radio
Played on.
It all happened so fast
And I could only see
The silhouette of his face
Between the shades.

I get dressed
With instant shame,
Regret, anger, and worry
That the word
Would spread
And my reputation
Ends on the grounds.
Who would've thought
That wanting a few kisses
Would end up in this?

Innocence is lost
With no knowledge
Or preparation,
With no awareness
Of the how and why
And the process
Or the consequences
Of the one minute
That changes a lifetime.

When there is no one
To educate or to trust,
It's hard to understand
Or predict the outcome
Of something so meaningful,
It's hard to understand
My role in this issue.
The question remains,
Am I the only woman
Or are there more
With the same problem?

April 15, 1983

Without Pity

The transparency
Of the rain
Made me
Remember you.
I saw your face
Serene and loving,
A smile
Was drawn
On your face,
My eyes
Gave you a look
Of bitterness.

I don't want
Fake feelings,
I don't want
Compassion,
I do not want love
Out of pity,
Because living loveless
Hurts to the deepest
And makes life bitter.

July 14, 1983

Rainy days

It's nice to walk
Under the drizzle
From your mate's arm
Sharing one umbrella
Making you feel
Like the princess
In the novella.

It's nice to daydream
On rainy days,
Work is tossed aside
Watching the raindrops fall,
Whispers and sighs
Are subtle,
And they all come
To the windows
To see what's happening.

It's nice to tell
The friends near
Of your crazy wants
And what you need.
It's nice to see
One of them gets up,
Opens the door
And invites you to walk
Under the rain with him.

It's nice to hear
The raindrops
Falling heavy
On the rooftop.

It's nice to see
It gets dark suddenly
But knowing we're safe
And we're together
Watching how the rain
Drenches all the plants.

It's nice to tell
Your mate
Of the enjoyment
Of listening
To the heavy raindrops
Over a sheet roof
Like in your memories.

It's nice to see
That your mate
Gets your hand
And directs you outside
To listen to the rain
From within the car.

The heavy drops
Fall over the sheets
Of a covered parking lot
And the shivers
Are from the cold,
And the smiles
Are from the memories
And the kisses
Are for the mate
That keeps you happy.

November 22, 1985

E M O T I O N S

Words learned,
Faces known,
Emotions stolen,
And feelings
Cleared
Inspire and provoke.

I learn,
I change,
I evolve.
As I learn,
I transcend
The norms
Imposed upon me,
I become free,
Into a butterfly
I transform.

Many Words

Many words
We say,
Many words
We feel,
We say much
Or we say
Not enough
To protect
Our hearts
From ail and pain.

Many words
We say,
Many words
We don't mean,
But we speak
To make others happy
As they hear
What they wish.

Many words
Hurt,
Many words
Kill the dreams
Of the person
Trying to be,
Many words
Praise
And many words
Don't say
Or mean anything.

Many words
We do feel,
Many words
We do not say,
For fear of harm,
We keep
Many words
Locked
In our minds,
Many words
We keep quiet
On our tongues.

February 13, 1990

My Solitude

Good day,
My solitude,
Here I am
Standing before you,
Basking
In your charms.

My beloved
Solitude,
My best friend,
My faithful companion,
Always sincere
And complying.

My solitude,
I've never felt
More in company
Than when I stare
In the face
Of nothingness,
Yes, my solitude,
I missed your whispers,
I missed your touch,
I feel fine here,
Here, I am myself.

My sweet solitude,
I missed you so,
Please –
No words,
I know I did wrong.
I thought

Love won it all,
However,
At times, I yearned
My isolation,
I missed my silence.

Oh, my solitude,
You're the one
That doesn't disappoint,
The one
That doesn't ignore,
The one
That doesn't deceive,
In your company
I have everything,
And, here,
I am the greatest lady.

July 31, 1989

Visions

I don't know
If I exist,
All I see
Are visions
Of abandonment,
People
Are not the same,
They don't smile,
Only feign,
They don't greet,
Only whisper
Words in shreds.

Visions
Of solitude
My eyes see,
A cruel world
Obstinate to please
Its wish
To do mean things,
Visions
Of dust
And filth
I see
Through my path,
Visions
Of hate,
Violence,
And selfishness
Among the crowds,

Tarnished visions
I see through
The diaphanous crystal
Of my remote
And darkened window
For fear of the company.

Visions
Of tragedy,
Of laments,
Of complaints,
Of envy
And indifference,
Today no one
Shows pity
Or patience,
There's no love,
People show
No conscience.

Visions
Of pain and grief,
My heart feels
As I see no one
Care for others
Unless it's
Practical
Or convenient.
The soul suffers,
The mind
Destroys itself
And no one sees
Or hears
The consequences.

Visions,
Visions,
That's what they are,
I don't know
If it's a dream,
I don't know
If it's real,
For this,
My own solitude,
I study the world
And its lack
Of affection,
In a more subtle
And clear way,
Critical visions,
Visions of life:
That's what they are.

March 14, 1990

My Will

When I die,
I want no
Meaningless words,
Double-edged smiles,
Sighs,
Or feigned tears,
Let it be all the same
As it was before,
Just as I lived it all.

I want no
Hypocrite eulogies
Full of lies,
Just to make me
Look good
Or your peace of mind.
– Say about me
And my true traits;
I was a loyal friend
Of pride
And stubbornness,
Of life itself
And no one else.
Whoever knows
Something about me,
Speak up
With no doubts or fear,
Don't lose the chance
To be the gossiper
And the spreader
Of untruths
And intimacies.

I want no
Black suits or veils,
I want outfits
In white, black, and red
Always in elegance
And simplicity;
White
For what I offered,
Black
For what I denied,
And red
For what I enjoyed.

With the music
Stand vigil over me,
For it made me happy
Over the years.
Sing to romance
And love,
I lived for them
And die with them
In my heart.

Don't bring me
Flowers
To wither with me,
Instead,
Grow them
For a new life,
To embellish
The earth
And bring joy
To the eyesight,
And me,
Just let me be.

I want my ashes
Kept in a gold box
Where everyone
Sees it,
Where everybody asks
Who I was.
I want my face
Painted in thousands
Of portraits
So I won't be forgotten.

I want to leave
The world a legacy,
Something personal,
A gift,
My mind in writing,
Words,
Paragraphs and sheets,
I kept hidden
Since my childhood.
I want my ideas
Divulged,
Perhaps I'll inspire
A hidden talent
And gets published
And thus,
Save the words
From the wind,
Oblivion,
And nothingness.

Don't cry
My departure,
I did what I wanted
And what I could
And I don't mind
The farewell.
Don't fight.
For what I leave behind,
Material things
Are not important
But the mentality is,
And that remains within.

To the Lord
I ask for forgiveness
For the teachings
I didn't follow,
I also apologize
To those whom I offended.

A new chapter begins,
I will be the main star
Where there are
No disturbances
Or sadness,
And peace
Always exists.

July 5, 1990

Regretful

Life fades away
In an instant,
And only
Memories remain.
Sad it is
To see the past
And realize
We didn't do
As we wished,
Sad it is
To see that life
Is a puff in a gift
And we don't seize
The joys
And the time
Offered to us.

I regret
Not helping
Or being present
When it was needed.
I regret accepting
And giving offers
Not really meant.
Today
We give away,
Tomorrow
We reproach,
And the next day,
We reclaim
What, as little or big,
We've given.

I still don't learn.
Because
Of my frustrations,
I curse my life,
My destiny,
My body,
My friends
And everything
In between.
Then, I repent,
I reconsider
And am grateful
For everything I have.

I regret
Not satisfying my life
At the right time,
Not satiating
My desires
In that precise moment,
Then it gets late
And everything seems
Undisposed.

Leave me alone
For a while
To appreciate
What I have
And what I threw away.

December 5, 1988

Alone

Let no one
Pity me,
Let no one
Feel sorry for me,
I can make it
On my own
With no requests
For anything.

I will struggle
Through life,
And nobody
Will defeat me,
I am sure of that,
I have to show
Those who believe
I am defeated,
That it's the opposite,
They do nothing
Without me.

One day
They see me suffer,
And the next,
As if nothing,
I smile.
And, no,
I don't fake
What I feel.

The failures
And sorrows
I carry alone,
In the success
They all join me,
To the birth
Of success
They all come,
But for the wake
And condolences
To the failures
No one shows up.

August 5, 1984

Who?

I go through life
Worried
Seeking the approval
Of others.
However,
Who cares about
My suffering?
They all ask
As a custom,
How are you?
But who stops
To hear the answer?

I have friends,
But when
I go to them,
Who listens to me
With attention
And interest
As I deserve?
Who wants
To understand me
As I have done
With them?

I know many
Look at me with pity,
But, who feels as I do?
They criticize, but,
Who offers me
Their advice
Or their help?

If I cannot move,
Who offers me
A hand
Instead of
Criticizing,
Instead of being
In the way?
If I cannot
Articulate
My thoughts,
Who has
The patience
To read my mind?
Who wants to lose
One minute
Of their time?

Others suffer
For seeing me suffer,
But only I – feel
What is inside,
And what happens
To me
And what I do
To live.
If I cry
Or if I am sad,
Who looks
Within me
To make me smile?
Few people,
Or no one,
Perhaps.

Let no one
Call me
A coward,
Or dumb,
Or useless,
Until someone
Puts himself
In my place
And sees
With my eyes
And feels
With my heart
The injustices
Of life.

February 17, 1989

Depression

How different
It was
A few months ago,
I used to laugh
Free and gladly
At anything
That came my way.
I was active
And full of energy,
I was beautiful
And felt loved,
I looked forward
To life,
I leaped
Through the days
Trying to get ahead.

Today
I drag myself
Out of bed
Only to land
On the chair,
I live in the past
And remember
Only what is sad,
The bad
And the useless,
My smiles are frowns,
I cry for no reason,
I sigh and yawn
And seek my isolation.

My beauty
Has disappeared,
The more I decorate
My face,
The uglier I feel,
I feel unwanted,
I don't want
To see anyone,
I don't want to speak
With anyone.
And I am
Always tired.

The springtime days
Mean nothing
Anymore.
How I envy
Others' laughter,
And yet,
I can't even smile,
But it seems
No one listens,
It seems no one sees,
It seems no one cares
About me.

March 20, 1990

Between Falls

Between falls
I thrive,
Some say I fall
Often, too much,
Yes, it's true,
I won't deny it,
Though I feel pain,
I force a smile
On my face
So that I and others
Will believe
Everything is great.

A fall,
In any sense,
Brings us down,
But it's the strength
And willpower
That counts
If we are to rise
And carry on
— And I don't stop.

A fall
Is a step back
And two steps forward,
Those who often fall,
Command the world
Because it's we
Who make changes
For a better life
And a better tomorrow.

I don't want
Pity,
I just want
Someone
To be there
And listen
To my pain,
Or, plainly,
Not be a hurdle,
So that when I fall,
I'll have plenty
Of space
Where to land.

July 9, 1985

56

I Will Win

I am going to win,
I will win the battle,
I will beat the odds,
The final war
Will favor me,
All will be
At my command,
And evil will ask
For my forgiveness.

I am going to win,
I swear,
I will come victorious
Out of this.
They will
Come to me
And I will assist them,
But whomever I see,
Instead of loving
Another,
They will love me.

I will see
My goal fulfilled
When I am
At the peak of success
Looking down
At those
Who were higher than me.

I will succeed,
I have to do it,
All alone,
I do not need
Anyone else,
I have the potential
To set goals
And fulfill them.

I will rid poverty,
Anyone
Can follow me,
And those
Who do not come,
I will leave behind
Where they want to be.

Childhood
Will be happy
And nothing
Will be dull,
Those of old age
Will need nothing,
They will have
Everything at hand.

I do not know where
Or even how,
But I will achieve it
With sacrifices
And nights
Of little sleep
And days of hunger.
That does not matter,
If the results
Will be splendid.

I will succeed,
You will see,
I fear nothing,
Yes, indeed.
Everything
Unpleasant
I leave behind.
I will succeed,
I will win,
There is no doubt
That I will do it
Alone and for me.
Wait patiently,
Soon you will see,
My dream, surely,
One day will come.

I will do it alone,
When I finish,
I will smile
Satisfied,
And will give a hand
To others
To follow
In my footsteps,
For me,
It is a privilege,
It is pride,
It's satisfaction
Of the soul
And mind.

July 11, 1984

I

It's good to know
Oneself
Inside and out,
To know
The weaknesses
And strengths,
To know
What we like,
What hurts
And bothers,
What we want
And search,
What we dream
And expect,
What we respect
Or tolerate.

In my work,
I am brave, audacious,
A bit philosophical,
A bit sane
And a bit crazy.
I am creative,
Self-analytical,
A perfectionist,
Determined,
Romantic, a dreamer,
Realistic and fanciful
And, why not?
Stubborn
And whimsical.

I am an observer
And intuitive,
With my friends
I'm sincere and direct,
I give my opinion,
At times exaggerated,
Honest and deliberate
Without fear
Of offending
Or losing anything
As I know it's appreciated
And respected.
At times I keep quiet
From what I know
And what I see
As I offend them
If I am truthful.

I am maternal
And protector,
I am faithful
And discreet,
A peacemaker
And counselor.
I am demanding,
Bossy but fair
And I act cautiously.
I am friendly
And trusting,
I do everything
For the friends
And I am a friend for life,
And though
They anger me,
I defend, help
And protect them.

I am always ready
To help and teach.
I try to forgive
And forget
When someone
Does me wrong,
As I know
I do wrong too.

I am sarcastic
And cynical
When the comments
Hurt me.
I am kind
And at times evil
But my actions
Are justified
Because it responds
To their actions.
I control my emotions
When I am attacked,
I control my reaction
When the problem
Is strong
And they expect me
To come undone.

I am strong
And rebellious
And raise my voice
To defend others,
When the attack
Is personal,
I keep quiet
And move aside
To not get things worsened.

I look for silence
And solitude
To meditate on my life,
In times of trouble
Or sadness
And be in peace
With myself.
I'm weak
In a strange environment,
In the middle
Of my frustrations
I feel alone,
I cry to relieve my soul.
Sometimes I ask,
Why me?
Though I know
We all have something
That doesn't fit in.

Of my persona,
I am proud,
A little conceited,
In my mirror,
I feel beautiful
And I am arrogant
Of my appearance,
And I am distinguished
When I speak.
In my characteristics,
I'm serious but happy,
I am quiet,
Sentimental, shy,
Noble, patient,
Considerate, pious
And understanding.

I know my virtues
Will take me far,
Modestly,
I feel superior
In smarts
But sometimes
I feel inadequate
Depending
On the situation
And people's attitudes.

I am conscious
Of my flaws
But I carry on.
I get up stronger
Of every fall
And, despite it all,
I think I am happy
And independent.
In my teenage life
I lived self-consciously,
But now, resignedly,
I live smiling.
I'm happy
With myself
No matter what happens.
I joke about myself
And of my failures
Because it's easier
Hear it from me
Before all other mouths.

I like routines
And stability
But I am also
Spontaneous and fun.

I'm not an angel
Nor holy
Or sanctimonious,
I am giving and selfish,
Complex
And simplistic.
I'm like everyone,
Good and bad,
But I am not vindictive
Or rancorous
And envy no one.

I like simple
And respectful people
Happy but peaceful,
Who reconsider
And improve
Their lives.
When I listen,
When I act,
I try to put myself
In their place
To feel
And see life
From their point of view.

I do not accept
What I do not give;
Betrayals
To my trust
And criticism
Behind my back,
Neither I accept
Lies, gossip
Or hypocrisy.

I am strong,
I fear nothing
But I fear old age
In loneliness
And oblivion.
I think I am a leader
And I lead
But in the end,
With no complaints
I follow all of them.
I have changed
With the times
And the experiences
But I hope
I'll always do my best
No matter with whom
Or the reasons to be.

April 14, 1989

Elopement

She eloped,
I got in trouble,
She did not obey,
I got the blame.

She's now free to do
And be out and about
But they keep
Close watch on me
And set rules
And boundaries.

She eloped
And I got the slap,
She then was pardoned
But I got the reprimands.

The elders cried
From hurt
And disappointment
That she eloped
And betrayed
Their trust
But I got warnings
And the punishment.

I listened to both sides,
I was the messenger
And the mediator
And did my best
To reunite them.
She made peace

With the elders
But they all forgot
Or don't see
That my intervention
Helped them
And for me
Things got worse.

She returned to her post,
She's, again,
The good caring daughter
And with a big stick
She orders, demands
And condemns.

She's on
Her high post
And I'm in trouble,
She's on their side
And they are with her,
But I have no status,
Control or power.

She became
The elders' eyes
And with authority
She uses her mouth
To judge my actions
As if she was pure,
Innocent and flawless
But, she's a sinner
And flawed like me
Or even worse.

I helped her
And supported her,
She was special to me
But now
She only sees
What she wants
And what I do wrong,
She doesn't see
Farther than her nose,
She doesn't remember
What she did,
She forgot her sins,
Such a good performer.

She could've
Offered me help,
Or at least,
She could've said
Something nice
To make my time
Less stressful
But she kept quiet,
Stern, disapproving
And at a distance
But when the time came,
She was ready
For the aggression.

It seems that marriage
Cleanses the body,
The behavior,
The mind and mouth
Of those who failed.
It seems that marriage
Makes any sinner
Holier than thou

And, perhaps, marriage
And children
Cause amnesia
As the sinner
Doesn't remember
All they ever did
In their younger days
But there's always
Someone
Who never forgets.

Don't give me
The short,
Sketchy story,
I know them all well
And I know what they did.
I'm not afraid to talk
And clear things up.
Long lost memories
Often are found
In the eyes
Of my biggest critics
Who pretend
To be honorable.

December 20, 1986

Admission

The vigilance
Was continuous,
The interrogation
Was frequent and direct,
The criteria, complaints
And reprimands
Were always
At the tip of the tongue,
The threats
And warnings
Were conflicting
But vague,
But the offer to help,
Listen or advice
Was never there.
The confidence
To ask or vent
Never existed.

My personal life
Was kept secret
Though it was part
And subject of complaints
But no one lives
A life laid bare
Or to the taste of others.
I lived a life
Pretending innocence,
Integrity and obedience
For the silent rules
That were never said
Or explained

But were understood
In the same manner.
Weakness and love
Made me sin,
I failed and failed big.
I failed and my secret
Will soon be exposed.

I can't bare it,
I want to vent
And be frank.
To avoid twice scolding,
I gather
The king and queen
To give them the news
Or a rude awakening,
I confess and admit
Of my big sin.
I broke the mirage
Of respect and honor
To traditions,
Customs and linage.

I cry from fear,
Culpability and shame,
I cry inconsolably
But no longer carry
The secrets in my head.
I feared repudiation,
I feared violence
But never suspected
The lord king,
Forceful and unpredictable,
Would support me.

Interrogations
Rain on me
But the tears
Don't let me speak
And the king
Defends me
Against her.
He protects me
From questioning
And comments,
He protects me
From the verbal whip
That lashes out,
He protects me
From demands
And explanations
That I cannot give.

Everyone shames
The family name,
Everyone breaks
With traditions
And expectations
But, in their eyes,
My actions
Are unspeakable
And look bad.

It hurts me to see
The disappointment
I caused them
And the anger
In their face
But having a child
Out of wedlock
Is not bad.

They point their finger
At me, I know,
Since it's a crime
Declared by the law
That protects men,
It's a flaw
Declared by the society
That never keeps quiet,
And the church
Brainwashes us
Inventing
Virtues and sins,
Heaven and hell
To keep us terrified.

I know I will be
The topic of gossip
For a long time.
I am not the only sinner,
But, being a woman,
I carry the weight
Of culpability,
Shame and sin
Like a cross
On my back
While men hide
Their misdeeds and sins
Under their feet.

October 30, 1990

E D U C A T I O N

Books,
Paper and pens,
Are the foundation
To understanding life
But paper and pens
Are the most important
Materials
For leaving your legacy.

Education
Is everywhere,
People
Are like weeds
With secrets
That nourish,
We all have
The potential
And beauty,
We are all
Teachers and students.

The Educator

From your patience
When teaching,
I have learned much.
What seemed indifferent,
Now I read
With pleasure.
Your lessons
Opened my mind
To other ideas,
To other opinions.
And all authors,
I respect greatly.

The criticism you gave,
In a positive manner,
Made me learn more.
At times, I answered
Erroneously,
But you disguised it.
Your explanations,
Clear and concise,
Emerge
With the precise nature,
Attracted
By a tender look
And a pretty smile.

Your interest
And sincere friendship
Brought me closer to you.
As a person and teacher,
You give

Your heart away,
In my eyes,
Makes you better
Than the rest.
I enjoy
Learning from you.
You're sensitive
To my faults,
And you understand
My thoughts
Without saying much.

Like a bird
Spreading happiness,
You spread drops
Of your knowledge
Above all minds
With pleasure
And harmony.
Your teaching
Is unconditional
And you
Don't expect rewards
For giving the world
The fundamentals.

Within you,
Teaching is a vocation.
You plant the seed
Of learning
In each student,
And this makes
For the elite
Of the future,
Who you, today,
Inspire confidently.

Your message,
With insistence,
Is nailed
Into my mind—
Save the intelligence
From the destructive
Ignorance.
Teacher today,
Teacher always.
Difficult, but gratifying,
Your work
Is always satisfying.
You are perfect for all
Who come to you,
Finding in you
The words of hope.

When you see
Their mentalities
Develop,
Feel proud,
You deserve it.
For all you have done,
And will do,
You should feel good,
Since few
Are like you
And because education
Is marvelous.

May 16, 1989

From Yesterday To Tomorrow

I've spent my life
Proving myself
To others
Despite the criticism
That impeded me
Everything.
Through my efforts,
I did something
Beneficial only for me:
I got an education.

I lingered
In the confinement
Of silence
For many years,
Searching through books
For words
That expressed
My insatiable desire
Of knowledge.

I have achieved
One more goal,
Today I graduate,
My dream
Is halfway accomplished.
My dreams of yesterday
Tomorrow will be true.
Today, I graduate,
Such pride for me,
How emotional it is,

But still,
I don't feel satisfied,
I know there's a lot
More ground to cover.
My true satisfaction
Will come,
Little by little, after this.

I got an education
With the belief
That I'd be better
Than before.
Although at times,
I had doubts,
I knew
I had to continue.
I knew my talents
Were exceptional
And of great help
To the formation
Of my future.

I sacrificed
Joyful nights,
Fun evenings,
And holidays
Locked up
With my books
By obligation
And my own choice.
The world moved
Around me,
But I sighed distractedly
And, returned
To my routine
Of endless reading.

I lost friends
Through the years,
Because of pettiness,
Ignorance,
Or misunderstandings,
I preferred my studies,
They chose
A moment of delight
And didn't understand
The importance
Of my school duties,
I could not conceive
Their empty lives,
Losing their time,
Their lives,
And their minds.

I got an education
To light up
My ignorance,
To save
My intelligence.
Although I got angry
For not having fun
As others did,
God gave me
Comfort and patience
To keep my routine.

I was blinded
By the pursuit
Of knowledge,
Amid letters and terms,
I learned to cultivate
Uncertainty,
Between this and that,

I learned to respect
Ideas, words,
And even the most
Absurd thoughts.

That window
That was closed
In silence,
Is one I can open now
To a happy noise.
I no longer worry
About people's uproar.
I have the degree
I deserve
Here in my hands,
The other things
Are not important,
My future has arrived,
My future is here.

I have my degree
As a reward
For nights of no sleep
And days
Of poor nutrition,
I am granted
The satisfaction
To be called an
Intellectual,
Who never gave up
In the face
Of any hardship.

Faith and sacrifices
Are paid off today.
Thanks to God
And the few
Who trusted me.
Sure of myself, I say,
What I learned well
Yesterday,
Tomorrow,
I will put into practice.

May 21, 1988

A Teacher

I wanted to be
A leader,
I wished to be
A positive
Role model,
In silence,
I begged to be
An inspiration
And I dreamt
Of changing
Someone life.

I coveted
Admiration
And respect,
I aspired to be
Someone special
Who has a voice
To share,
I pleaded
That I'd be taken
Into account
And I needed to leave
Traces of me
Where I touched
The ground.

I looked
For gratitude
In a smile.
I asked to be
The heroine

Of the story
And save
Someone's mind
So I decided
To be a teacher,
A teacher
Of ordinary life.

I wanted to teach
Through
What I have lived
And be the model
Of what worked
Or failed,
I wanted to prevent
Other's falling
Like I did
So many times before,
So I picked up
The paper and pen
And began to write down
My philosophies
And my poems.

July 11, 1990

Between The Books

I am a learner
From school books
And my classes,
From the streets
And incidents,
And from social
And family gatherings.
I am a learner,
No matter what I do
Or where I go,
I am a learner
And a teacher too.

Between the books,
Between the pages
Or between the stacks,
I experience
The highs and lows,
The permissible
And the forbidden,
The amusing
And the sadness,
Moments of peace
And episodes of wars,
I feel loved,
Loveless and unloved.
It's a cycle
And a routine,
Between the books,
I learn and grow,
Between the books,
I've become an adult.

I get up at dawn
Feeling tired
From doing homework
That never ends.
I get ready,
Looking pretty,
And with a door slam,
I run down the stairs,
I leave in a rush
But my feet
Get tangled up.

Between rows
Of apartments,
I have to open
And close
Various gates
And make many turns
But off to school
I go.
The sun,
Always in my eyes,
Dazzles me
So crestfallen
I walk on the street
The heavy backpack
On my shoulder
Make me lose
My balance
But somehow,
I hold up
And I go on my way,
I can't take the luxury
To be late.

I jaywalk
Cautiously,
To save time
And many steps.
I go up and down
The central divider
As fast as I can
But it gets
More complicated
Every time.
How I wish
There would there be
Metal poles
On both sides
To hold on to
And ease the crossing.

The traffic passes
And while I wait
To cross,
Someone yells out
My name,
The horn beeps,
I hear compliments,
Flirty and approving
Whistling
And, even though
It's for a moment,
It makes me smile
That someone
Notices me
Even if from afar
But it angers me
That nobody stops
To give me a ride.

Finally,
I get to my class
Ready to take a nap,
As much as I want
To keep awake,
I can't.
The professor's
Monotonous voice
Puts me in a trance.
I spend the time
With my eyes half open
Though the lecture
Seems interesting.

It's the same thing
In all my classes,
Take notes,
Read books,
Give oral and written
Presentations
But math
Is not my cup of tea.
The only class
I found fascinating
Was creative writing
Where I went happily
And without fail.

I rush
From place to place,
I walk all day,
I hurry
For my next class
But I'm still always late.
College life is stressful
And a nuisance,

I dream of the day
When I have
My home office
And spend time writing
From the inspiration
I see out
Of my window.

I walk all year long,
In times of rain,
I end up soaked,
On windy days,
The gusts
Push and pull me
And I feel vulnerable.
In hot weather,
There's nowhere to hide
From the sun
That hurts my skin
And in times
Of intense cold,
My bones
Are more brittle
And rigid
Then I knew.
The freezing cold
Weighs on me
As I move
And it irritates me
To have to walk
When I can't.
How I wish to have
A tiny convertible
That'd fit anywhere
To prevent problems
Of the weather.

Sometimes
I eat something
In the cafeteria
But sometimes
There is no time
Or there is no money.
On the way back home,
I walk slow pace
As I feel a pain
On my side
From hunger
Or just air.
To make matters worse,
Between each step,
I make up recipes
To cook
When I get there.

I count the steps
To see
If I arrive any sooner,
I count the minutes
To turn the TV on,
Enjoy my seat,
Relax
And nap for a while.
As I walk,
I tell myself stories
That make me laugh
But I cough
To dissemble
For the people
Who may look at me
Through their windows.

Sometimes
Walking back home
Is more tiring
Than walking around
The school
Or maybe,
It all adds up,
But I stop
To take a breath.
I turn back to see
The distance
I've walked
And what's still left
To reach my apartment
And feel protected
In my element.

Another day
And week,
Another month
And year
That go by.
I come home
And on my table,
I see pens and markers,
Handwritten notes
And binders.
Some books are open
And others are shut
On a high stack
Against the wall.

Seems I've made
A collection
Of text books,
Seems that the books

Tell me
That between the pages
And each and every book
I studied from
Are the troubles
I've lived
As a woman,
As a family member,
As a student,
And as a friend.
Seems the memories
Come alive
Just at the mere sight.

Between the books,
Classes
And assignments,
Is my life, simple,
Yet, complicated,
By the characters
That contribute
Or create incidents
And situations
I dreaded
Or never expected.

Between the pages
Of the books I read,
I found inspiration
And strength
To look at me
And give the next step.

May 1, 1990

Diploma

Graduation came
With a certain distress
Of the, 'Now what?'
And limitations,
Complications
And much doubt
Of my persona
Surge about.

I see the diploma
In my hands
And I see its meaning,
It reminds me
That my beau
Walked me
Down the aisle
To get the diploma
Because my body
Doesn't function
Under watchful eyes
Of stressful events.
The diploma
Is there to be hung
To decorate
The empty wall,
It is to remember
All the noise
Of clapping, cheers,
Handshakes
And happy voices
In approval
Of the accomplishments.

The diploma
Is to remind me
Who I am
And what I wanted
To be.
It's there
To remind me
Of the struggles
And dreams
And how far
I've come
And how far I can go.

It's a reminder
Of the hunger
And thirst,
Of the solitude,
The plentitude
And nothingness,
It's a reminder
Of the worries
About everything
And the laughter
I released
In moments of peace
And of the tears I shed
When I felt weak.

It's a reminder
Of all the rushing
From place to place
And thing to thing
And how time
Stood still
When I wanted it
To end.

It's a reminder
Of the mental
Overworking
And the headaches
I got.
It's a reminder
Of the many times
My body
Couldn't function
But my mind
Kept pushing me
Up and out
And when my mind
Was defeated,
My body was ready
To spring up.

The diploma
Reminds me
Of the bad,
Embarrassing,
Good and happy
Experiences.
It's a reminder
Of my weaknesses,
Whims and defeats.
It's a reminder
Of my persistence,
Of an accomplishment
And bravery
To face uncertainty.

The diploma
Is a reminder
Of all the friends
I made and lost
But their company
And their words
Enriched my life
And helped to shape me.
Is a reminder
And proof
That some teachers
Paid attention
And showed interest
In my strong points
And their encouragement
Made the difference
For me to see
What was a hobby
Can become a profession.
The diploma
Is a reminder
Of all the knowledge
I attained
But, at what cost?

December 7, 1990

REMEMBRANCE

The history
And mixed cultures
Are enlivened
By traditions
Of past living
Are remembered
With pleasure
And yearning.

There must be
Remembrance onward.
Our steps,
Our actions,
Our words,
Must show
Pride and respect
For our roots
And for the new culture
That comes to be
So new generations
Will succeed.

Enemies Of Race

The more
You hurt me,
The stronger I become
That's a given fact
Of life.
Once, I was vulnerable
But today,
I have a strong mind.

Please,
Don't hide it,
I know you dislike me,
You tolerate my being
Out of compassion,
But your indifference
Makes you inferior
In my eyes,
Your supremacy
Is only fear hidden away.

I have mixed blood.
Don't you?
I am part Indian,
Proud of my heritage.
Are you totally pure?
Are you proud
Of your heritage
As I am of mine?

I am proud
Of my origin,
I don't forget my culture,

I don't hide
Behind a fake name.
Don't tell me
You're better,
Show me
With your actions,
And your thoughts.
Show me when others
Have your acceptance
And respect.
When others feel
Equal to you,
You will have respect too.

In an oversight
You took away my land,
But never my dignity,
You believe me a slave
Because
I am peaceful,
But if you think
About it,
I have a stronger
Command
Because you live
In constant fear
Of my rebellion.

I came here
As a migrant
Within my own land
Of a continent,
The land of my ancestors.
You crossed barriers
And oceans
To reach your destiny.

You invaded my land,
Stole my goods
And dominated my people
With whips,
Guns and bibles.
Now,
I work for you,
And you mistreat me.
Could you take it
If you were
In my place?

You discriminate
Against me
Until I put an end to it
With the power
Of my truth
And the strength
Of my fist.
Then you'll know
I am first and last.
You'll cry regretting
When you see
Yourself lost
But I won't listen
To your pleading,
As you do with me.

Racism
Is an immature mentality
Fearful of losing
A place
You never had.
Your blood
Doesn't make you better,
It makes you fearful

With a step
I can get ahead,
It is fear of losing
The stolen place,
It's fear of losing
The domain you've gained
With my tears, sweat,
Blood and my land.

You forbid
People of my race
An education
And liberty,
While you profit
From our poverty.
If you have to keep
The masses
Quiet and humble,
Then,
Your foolish mentality
Shows
You're not as smart
As you perceive to be.

Think
Of the consequences
Of your discrimination,
And put things
To a halt
While you are in control.
One day,
Maybe soon,
The tables will turn
And you will see
Yourself on the ground
Then,

You will become
The sufferer,
The unwanted
And the minority,
Ignored.

Be a good example
Of well-being,
Let the truth be told
Of your forefathers
But search for peace
And equality
For all the children
Before it's too late.

May 3, 1989

My City

In my city,
The women,
With their shawls,
Are culturally
Different,
And the men,
With their hats,
Are true gentlemen.
They have built cities
With their blood
And sweat.

My beautiful city,
Made in years past,
A mixture
Of cultures,
Races and tongues,
You are also young,
Happy
And distinguished.

They rebel
Against a past
That is extinguishing.
Your speed
Along the path
Of each day
Is felt and noted,
But a slow pace
Of life is also maintained.
People enjoy
But do not give up.

My city,
The nights
Look like days
With such lighted
Boulevards, avenues
And freeways

My city
Shines at night,
It wears a mask,
Ready
For what will come,
Each dawn
Brings new hope
Of a better life.

August 9, 1983

My Two Nations

I am Chicano,
A product
Of two countries,
I am
From two cultures,
I have two mixed
Languages,
I belong to Mexico
From heart and soul,
I am here, by choice.

I possess
Mexican heritage,
In my veins,
Mixed blood
Runs freely with grief
But shows sympathy,
My race is brave
Although it's humiliated
By the gringos
Who do me evil
And Mexico
Who believes me a stranger.
We plant
But don't cultivate,
We are rejected
Here and there,
To both countries
I prove I know
Both cultures
And I am better
Than them.

In the corners
Of my home,
The mask falls off,
I free my soul,
I sing the chronicle
Of my life and my race.
A friendly hand
Educated me,
As so many times
I joined my father,
And with pleasure
We labored in the fields
That feed our dreams.

I am Indigenous,
Dark, burned
From so much sun,
My body suffers
The changes
Of the weather
Working
Other people's lands
Sprinkled with the tears
Of my laments.

I have left my life
In each piece of land,
We have spread out
In territories
Of the North
And we rooted
Descendants
Between two seas
And borders.
We give ourselves
The support needed

To start each day
Because no one
Sees us or hears us.

We want possession
Of what was ours
Back in the day.
We work the land
With pride
And dedication,
Watching the seed,
That will feed our hearts,
Grow and spread out
To other lands.

This is the finale
Of my confession
For those who live
In my two countries,
— My nations.
Today and always,
I will struggle with them.
For my people
I will reconcile
With them
Sacrifices, I will prosper.
My children will have
What I only dreamt.

March 10, 1983

D E D I C A T I O N S

No matter
How serious
Or strong,
Enduring or close,
Relationships
Have made me
Who I am.

I am grateful
For each one of them,
As I taught,
I learned,
Unknowingly,
That we all search
For acknowledgment.

Friendships

Friendships arise
Anywhere,
With anyone,
For any reason,
In any time
And for whatever
Length of time.

Some friendships
Are strong
And make you see
The best of you,
With a few words
They lift
Your self-esteem,
They stick with you
And see you
Through your points
Of highs and lows
Anguish, whims,
Failures, rewards
And miseries.

Friendships
Come and go
But some remain
In your memories
Because
In a special way,
They contributed
To making you
Who you are.

True friendships
Listen and observe,
As an outsider
But push
And encourage
As part
Of oneself
And they give you
Their point of view
To the problems
You're living.

True friendships
Don't leave us wishing
They had listened
And encouraged us,
They don't leave us
Wishing
They had told us
The mistakes
Of our choices,
They don't leave us
Wishing
They had given us
The strength and logic
They promoted
To others.

December 15, 1990

Maria

Maria,
Woman of white skin,
Your eyes
Are two stars.
Your face
Reflects harmony,
Your smile is sweet,
And your laughter
Freely exhibits.

I admire
Your simplicity
And respect
Your kindness,
You're a strong woman
In the face
Of frustration,
At the same time,
Sensible
And sentimental
In the face of love.
You're a woman
And child,
Sophisticated
And humble,
Frivolous, dominant,
And kind,
In your heart,
Love
Is always beating.

Without any doubt,
You take charge
Of what is around
Or before you.
You offer
Your hand frankly
And never
Have enough
Of other's problems.
You are special,
You became
An angel
And dictator
Of my actions,
I thank you
That, at every moment,
You took care of me.

Maria,
Romantic woman,
Sentimental poet,
Your dreams
Will come true,
Since God
Takes care of you.

April 3, 1983

Friends We Were

I helped you
Before you asked,
I offered you
What I had
Before it was needed,
I opened my heart
And home,
I exposed my life
And I risked it all.
Now you
Set me aside
Like any stranger
I was not.

I believed
You were a loyal friend
In the good
And bad times,
Together,
Or for our lives,
A little apart.
But no,
You're as cold as clay.

I protected
And defended you
Like an unsheltered
Child.
I did not expect
Anything from you,
I just listened,
I gave my advice,

Thinking
Of your welfare
When
You couldn't think.

You'll realize,
From all your friends,
I gave you a hand,
I was always ready
For anything
In your problems,
Without any doubt,
For our friendship
Of years past.

In this mess
I don't lose,
My heart is at peace,
By helping you,
I did a favor
To the world
As I cared for you
With no fears.

I gave you all
Within my reach,
And now
That I'm not needed,
You discard me
Like a Kleenex.
I gave you
The best of me,
I wanted
To see you happy,
Now you betray me
Judging how I am.

It came as a surprise
To find out
You talk about me.
Don't make excuses,
For pity or grief,
From this experience,
I've learned to know
Humanity.
I wish you the best,
If a man
Can break
This friendship,
I no longer worry.
I did all I could,
And you,
Better than anyone,
Should know that.

After defending
And protecting you,
You ignore
And criticize me,
And, they even say,
You hate me,
It hurts,
But you'll suffer
The consequences.

I won't be there
Next time
You need a friend,
And no one will do
What I did for you,
Not your man,
Or your next friend
Will give all of itself

To know
What makes you suffer
Or makes you happy.

With our separation
You lose
The confidant,
The adviser,
And the one
Who got nothing
In return.
You lose
Your best friend,
From you, I learned,
That true friendship
Doesn't exist,
Friendship
Is only for a time
And issue
That unites
And guides us ahead.

I ask only one thing:
Don't tell anyone
Our intimate secrets,
Not because I fear
What is said
About me,
But so people
Will consider you
A good friend.

September 8, 1989

Little Princess

Dressed
In innocence,
Stop before me,
Smile,
And don't deny
Your feelings,
Show your beauty
As it is,
And for a moment
Forget your modesty.

Walk slowly,
Smoothly
And melodiously
Among the aisles
Of chrysanthemums
And carnations,
Smile proudly
And look around,
People admire
Your charms and youth.

Magical girl,
Like a dove
You want to fly,
When the bells
Strike six o'clock,
Before the altar
You'll be blessed,
The angels are joyful
And in chorus
They praise you.

As special lady
You are,
The birds
Will raise you
Without doubt,
Or worry,
For your virginal
Candor.
The chirping
Of the goldfinches
Make a pulsating echo
Inside and outside
The chapel
And all for you,
Beautiful little princess.

Little princess
Of fifteen years,
Your youth is learning
That shines on your life,
Like the butterfly
That flies to the light.

Fifteen springs
Are yours today,
Feel like the master
Of the world,
Feel like the master
Of all things,
Close your eyes
And let yourself move
To the rhythm
Of the music,
Dance to the compass
Of the waltz
That was composed

For you.
Revolve
On the dance floor
And let
Your innocence show,
Your naïve life
Is a virtue,
Enjoy,
This is your day.
The beautiful fantasy
Makes of this,
A captivating night.

Little princess
Of only fifteen years,
Young and beautiful,
Today you begin
A voyage
That'll take you
Among the stars
And seas,
Between the sun
And moon.
Enjoy
What waits for you.

May 27, 1989

To You

To you,
My dear friend,
As time passed,
I came to know you,
And now I know
How you feel.
As days went by,
I learned
To love you,
I admire
Your decisiveness,
I respect
Your strong
Character,
You are unique,
And in my life
You have
A special place.

My heart
Opened to you,
And I smiled,
Your comforting
Words,
Made me forget
My pain,
I denied my sadness
To you
So your happiness
Would not fade away
But you
Always asked,

What is wrong?
I answered,
It is nothing important,
Between
Whispers and sighs,
But everything ended up
In a confession.

You have heard
My lamentations,
You heard
My problems
As no other has,
And we shared
Our happiness.
Together
We have laughed,
Together
We have cried,
For this
And much more,
I thank you
For such
Important moments
We have shared.

To you,
My dear friend,
For letting me see
In your heart
The kindness
Of the man you are.
Your beautiful words
Shined
Through my life
In the darkest

Times,
You gave me peace
And the strength
To carry on.
Because of you,
I feel loved,
You read my thoughts
And give me support
To keep at it
And improve.

I was always
At your level,
I helped you,
You helped me.
Inseparable we were.
For you, I felt jealous,
Jealous of your time
And the attention
You gave to others
And I thought
You were forgetting me.

The trail
We have walked
Has ended,
We must bid farewell.
Do not stop to think
Of what you leave behind,
Life has to go on
And you lose time
Looking back
At what has passed.
Carry on,
And don't stop for anything,
I plead.

Today
We say farewell,
Tomorrow
We will remember
Happily
The good times
And, sadly,
The bad ones too,
But I will
Remember it all.
Here are no promises,
Here are no oaths,
Only sincere
And feelings
Of affections.

May 20, 1983

Forgotten Friendship

Strange is life,
Yesterday we were
Undivided friends,
Today we are
Plain acquaintances.

But I thank you
For all you did
For me,
You lifted me up,
You encouraged me,
Never will I forget
That, because of you,
I am who I am.

Would it be
You changed
Of idea
What was
Our friendship,
Or, for me,
Yours
Is no longer
The same?

Today
You're bound
To others
And I,
—I am independent.
I'm not hurting,
I'm not worried,

My happiness
Is from within
And gives me peace,
And this is reflected,
Certainly, in the sight,
Bright eyes
And smiling face.

Today,
We just say
Hello and goodbye
As custom,
Compromise,
Or for fear
Of what others
Would say.
Don't feel obligated
Towards me,
I am happy as I am,
And I'm not doing
Badly at all.

April 2, 1987

White Beauty

I had a friend
With white
Beautiful hair
And the bluest
Piercing eyes
That penetrated
To my soul.

He was a youngster,
He needed time,
Attention, care,
Activities and games
To be entertained,
Even if he was mellow,
Quiet, loyal
And affectionate.

It only lasted
A few weeks
But, for a time,
I had someone
Who was eager
To see me.
I was happy
To come home
And find him
Waiting for me
Out on the balcony.

I came home ready to flop
On the bed
But he required

Going for walks.
I wasn't accustomed
To anyone
Depending on me
And this
Gave me more problems.

I also knew well
This tiny apartment
Wasn't for the both of us.
I knew my friend
Needed space to play,
To walk, run and grow,
Space where
He'd have his bed,
His toys
And his bowl.

With grief in my heart,
I gave away
My Alaska husky,
A white beauty,
And it hurt
Never giving him a name
And not taking his picture
But he was rehomed
With family members
That wanted him
Only to be lost
Forever.

November 20, 1986

Rosa

I met
My great friend
In fourth grade
And we became
Inseparable
Until the high school
Graduation day.
There were
Intermissions
As she's younger
But the phone calls
Brought us up-to-date.

In every chance
We had,
We spent it together
With the other girls
Who followed us.
We were two
Innocent creatures
But,
How comforting
And pleasing it was
To have my friend
By my side.
With her next to me,
I felt strong,
I felt defiant
And complete.

The greatest friend
Of my youth
Was gentle
And kind-spirited.
She knew my secrets
And fears
But there was loyalty.
We understood
Each other well,
I raised her mood
And told her
All the good things
I saw in her
And she raised
My self-esteem.

My friend Rosa,
With her face
Always smiling,
Was my strength
And good company
In recess.
With her hand
Always assisting,
She was my helper
When I decided
To give poetry a try.
With her step
Always patient,
She was my support
In a thousand ways.
With her words
Always encouraging,
She was my adviser
When I needed
To be heard.

With her ear
Always attentive,
She was my audience
When I wanted
To laugh and talk.

Such a nice surprise
To see her in college,
Even if only
For a semester
But I felt happy
To have her
By my side.
I made her part
Of my group of friends
And we shared
Good times
And all the problems
We had as adults.

The university
Separated us,
She chose a job,
I chose my studies.
How I wished
She had been close to me,
I know my life
At the university
Would've been
Less frightening
If she had been present.

When our life
Is in turmoil,
We realize
The mistakes made
Of not appreciating
Those we had close
When given the chance.
I know I failed her
For not keeping
In contact
But between books,
Homework, classes
And real-life problems,
There was no time
For friends,
And that is my regret.

I don't remember
If I ever thanked her
For being my friend
Or ever said
All she means to me
And I am sorry
For that too
But I want her to know
She is very much missed.

November 20, 1990

IN GENERAL

There are words,
Memories
And facts
That don't fit
Anywhere
Specific
But must be
Told and kept
For the importance
Of the people
And the old days.

The Calling

Like the whispering
Of the trees
As the leaves move,
I whisper to you,
Softly but firmly,
The sadness
Of this farewell.

A kiss and a hug
I leave you
As memories,
This farewell
Is difficult,
Your eyes show
Crystal tears,
In my heart
I feel the sharp pain
Of death.

The importance
Of this love
Is reflected
In the sky,
The clouds
Have turned gray,
So I cry silently
While you look
Downward
In fear of loneliness.

The echo of eternity
Is calling,
My body turns cold,
My soul feels warm
And my eyes open up
To the surprises
He has prepared for me.

Whisper with sighs
The sincerity
Of your feelings,
Tell me
You'll love me
Tomorrow,
I need this belief
In my mind
To help me
Through the waiting
Until the echo
Of eternity
Calls you too.

I'll go up slowly
Through the clouds
Of cotton,
I will linger
In the place
Where I can grab
The air
And verify the truth
Of my visions.

March 28, 1989

The Madness Outside

Close the door,
The stagnant noise
From outside,
Is unbearable.

The madness,
The insensibility,
Has made me cry
Enough.
My soul
Can no longer
Tolerate it.

Close the door
To the madness
Outside.

February 15, 1990

The Bus

I started
My college years
In the agricultural valley
Where I live.
Long before there was
Public transportation,
A clunky school bus
Made its rounds
Throughout
To pick up the students
Very early
And return them
In the evenings.

The bus was a relic
From decades past
And the white dull paint
On the outside
Chipped away easily,
Only the logo
And the school's name
Were in good shape.

It picked me up by 6:30
And the sun on my face
Made me squint
Giving me the look
Of being angry
But, in truth,
I was afraid
And felt isolated.

On the first day,
A strange sensation
Came to me,
The doors opened up
And I saw myself
As a child,
Holding on tight
To the railing
To climb the high steps
Of the bus
That now
Takes me to college.

The first seat
By the entrance,
Became mine
And I saw the faces
Of who got on next.
Through the big window,
I enjoyed the view
Of the familiar route
But looked nice
And interesting
With that early dew
Although we bounced
Onto the worn out
Hard seats
From the holes and bumps
On the streets.

The driver
Was still young,
Handsome, friendly
And always happy.
His conversations
With the others

Were entertaining.
Just as I got in,
He turned the radio on
To the music in trend.
The ride to school
Gave me time
To appreciate the songs
And pay attention
To the rhythms.

Sometimes,
We hit the red light
Before making a turn
Towards the college
And I had time
To admire
The statue of a mother
Walking hand in hand
With her children.
In the other corner
Was an outdoor clock
And the time told me
If I was all right
Or if I had to rush.

I kept quiet
And looking down
The first days
But when it was time
To get off at the school,
I heard caring voices
Telling me,
Be careful!
Everyone rushed
And I didn't pick out
Faces and voices

But I thought,
If they are concerned,
They must be good people
And can be good friends,
But I wasn't courageous
To initiate anything.

My first friend
Introduced herself
And I began to lose
My shyness.
I no longer felt
Out of place,
With chats and glances,
I began to see others
Like me, shy, quiet
And serious
And made the effort
To make everyone
My friend.

Now that I had
People to talk to
And a reason to laugh,
I couldn't help
Being loud at times.
In the mornings,
When I got on the bus,
I heard people
Kind of waking up
And straightening
Themselves
But someone yells,
'Here comes Giggles,'
And the chit chats
Began all around.

In the evenings,
I looked forward
To the rides
Although
They seemed shorter,
But we were relaxed
And talkative.
How I wished
I lived farther away
To continue
With the conversation
And the enjoyment.

I also had some
Serious talks
With my bus mates
and got to know
Everyone intimately.
I asked a young man
About his mother,
The response was
She was unwell
And turned away
To hold in his tears.
I wanted to hug him
In support,
But the backseat
And my inhibitions
Were in the way
So a smirk
And a light caress
On his hand
Made him understand.

The bus
Broke down often

Although
It never left us stranded.
To our discontent,
The bus had a twin
With only more cushiony
But slippery seats
And it was proven
One spring morning.
I got on so happy
And sat behind the driver
Next to my friend,
I talked and giggled
So flirtatiously
But, as we turned,
I slipped off the seat
And ended up
On the floor.
The comments, the laughter,
The helping hands
Came fast
But nothing relieved
The embarrassment.

Those holidays
When the driver predicted
Few students
Were riding back,
We had a van
Or a mini-bus
And the bus and us
Became the joke
For some of my friends.
Of course,
I defended the bus,
The people and the rides.

Nobody knew
But for two years,
The rides
In the school bus
Were part of my well-being.
My happy mind
Started every morning
With lots of smiles
And greetings.
The rides gave me
Time to relax,
The passenger mates
Helped me feel
Optimistic.
As I was acknowledged,
I felt positive
About myself
Every moment.

After I transferred
Schools,
The college
Made big changes
And it was sad to learn
It removed the school bus
As public transportation
Took over countywide.
But it's not the same
As riding the bus
Full of students,
Peers and friends
Where we can joke,
Chat and know each other
In comfort.

I feel truly lucky
To have ridden
The school bus
As it gave me
A chance to meet
Some great people
That made great friends
Who, unknowingly,
Helped me
With my self-esteem.
The school bus
Also gave me a chance
To make dreams
And great memories.

In analogy,
On the highway of life,
You are either,
the driver or the passenger.
You drive forward
Or, for a moment,
Stay in neutral
But you don't go
In reverse often.
And you drive
In slow motion
Or go full speed
Picking up or dropping off
Faces and emotions
In its due time
Of our lives.

In analogy,
You look at life
Through the big window
From the front seat

To see what's coming up
Or you try to peek
Through
The small windows
On the sides
As we only use
The back windows
In emergencies,
And to see
What's left behind.

In analogy,
The size of the bus
Is the room we furnish
And the space
We fill and hoard
With baggage, packages
And junk
And within us,
It's all the emotional
Overload we carry
With useless memories
That takes us nowhere.

March 10, 1985

Autumn

Strolling
Through the park,
I see the trees
From the trees
To change colors.
I feel the cold
Winter's air,
An air of nostalgia,
An air of yearning,
An air of burned-out dreams
And solitude.

Beautiful blue sky
With clouds
Of cotton
Over the birds
That have not left,
Still sing
Among some flowers
That summer left behind
And start building
Their nest.

People walk
Hurriedly to their lives
And I sit and note
My observations.

October 15, 1983

The Dorm

On the second floor,
In the middle
Of the hall
And overlooking
The street little traveled,
Was my room
That became my house
The first year
At the university.

It was a strange place
And I felt alone
And frightened.
In school, I felt lost
And barely functioned
But in my room,
The tears of weakness
Flowed freely.
I wanted to escape
From this place,
I wanted to escape
From these feelings
That were not understood.

The environment
Was kind of gloomy
As I felt like a prisoner
Under the timer
And guards keeping watch
At every turn.
It was an environment
Of individualism

And loneliness
Where each
Defend for themselves
And no one cares
Of their neighbors.
It was a depressive
Environment
That never had
The feeling of home
And the musty smell
Was impregnated
On the floors.

It was an environment
Of rectitude
Where we must
Keep vigilant, obedient
And disciplined,
Where the rule
Was to live
Under locked doors
And silence at all costs,
It didn't matter
What time it was
But any noise and lights
Must be off at ten.

I felt as if I was
A long-time resident
In a hospital
Where visitations
Are the entertainment
But are allowed
Only on certain
Times and days.
It was an environment

Of schedules
Even for the cafeteria.
It was an environment
Of distaste
As the food served
Had no flavor at all.
I felt like a child
Needing the protection
Of the family
But there was no one
To give me a hand
Or to make my time
Any better.

Memories came alive
Of a childhood
I pushed aside.
I wept
By the window
Of my room
In the second floor
Wishing those people,
Who looked so small
Walking outside,
Didn't left me behind.
The same feelings
Of loneliness,
Abandonment
And impotence,
Enveloped me again.
Now I was in conflict
With being a grown-up,
Wanting to be independent
And resenting
The absence.

Stress, loneliness,
Fear and depression
Invaded my mind
And my environment
And were confounding
With my physical health.
A weird incident
Happened in the shower.
I fainted one morning
In autumn.
No one heard the thump,
No one interrupted
The blackout.
The faint
Turned into a dream,
As the water hit my face
And my head covered
The drainage,
I saw myself
In the first
And third person
Looking at a waterfall
Nearby.
I was a horse
Drinking water
By the river shore.
The water was clear
And peaceful.
I turned to the sky
And I saw the sun
Dazzling me
And the same glare
Made me wake up
And come back to life.

Each night,
Inside my room,
As I turned off the light,
I had a sensation
That someone
Was behind me
With a knife in hand
Ready to stab me
In the back.
When sleeping,
I tried to relax
But had nightmares.
Was it me
Or was it this place?

I regretted
Being at this school
If I wasn't prepared
For these changes.
I wished to go back
To previous
Times and places
When things
Were simple and fun,
When I was happy
To be me
And I had friends.

Looking for relief,
In front of my bed,
With the rosary at hand,
I knelt and started to pray,
Repeat and repeat,
Count and repeat,
Then I lost count,
I got confused.

In the end, I prayed
Directly to God,
My prayers became
My words of need
And cleared my feelings.
I asked for strength,
Compassion
And guidance
To all my fears
As loneliness
Is dubious and tricky.

I closed my eyes
And the tears flowed
Like a wild river.
Between my prayers,
I felt a white veil,
So light, soft,
And warm,
Coming down
From heaven
To cover me.
I felt protected,
The tears flowed
But I felt mental relief
And a load off of me.
I felt
In another dimension
Until the phone rang
And it brought me
Back to life.

With time,
My fears subsided
Or the evil spirits
Flew away.

The girls next door
Became my friends
Although never as close
Or for an extended time
As the ones, I had before.

I only tolerated
One year
In this environment
And my dorm room,
A place
That was scheduled
And guarded
Like a prison
And with a depressive
Ambiance
Like a hospital.
A place
That was my hospital,
My madhouse
And my prison
In my mental state.

July 20, 1986

Studio 251

When the roommates
Have a different
Lifestyle,
When their guests
Are not to my satisfaction
And when problems
Arise out of nothing,
It's time to pack up,
It's time to make peace
And move out.
Before ending
As enemy mates,
Is best to be neighbors
And leave the hate.

And so studio 251
Became my home
For some years,
A tiny apartment
On the second floor
With a nice view
To the courtyard
Overlooking a lake
Where many ducks
Swam, bathed,
Sang and ate.

Few people went out
To their balconies,
Few people were outside,
Few people used the pool,
Few people made noise,

Few people walked by.
Everyone lived
Very privately and hidden,
We all lived for us
And didn't acquaint
With the neighbors
For anything.

My door opened
To few visitors
But, even so,
I was called a libertine
To my face
But laughed
At my despair.
Others chose hypocrisy
And, behind my back,
Worded dissatisfactions
Of me
Causing problems
And embedding on the weak
Doubts of my integrity
Until they achieved
What they wished.

The true character
Of my identity
Revealed in my solitude,
With no makeup,
No words, no fantasies,
No eyes on me.
And studio 251
Was my cave, my escape
And my refuge
Where I did not see,
Did not hear

And did not speak
With anybody for days.
The silence
Within my walls
Was broken at times,
By the footsteps
On the stairway
For the neighbor
Or by the ducks outside.

The friends I had
Were for school time
But when
It became necessary,
Looked for my help,
My company
And my protection.
Yes, the same ones
Who contributed
To my anger before,
Later needed me
And I housed them
All the same.
Studio 251,
Was also their escape
Though at different times
And circumstances.

The empty walls
Of my studio
Witnessed my eagerness
To see the man I love
Only to quickly
See me cry
From a barrage
Of accusations

And insults
During the arguments
About nothing
And broke me
Into million pieces.
The empty walls
Witnessed a relationship
Coming undone
And the unrivaled pain
Left within
And the self-blame
That dwelled there.

Pressures
From every point
Brought me ill-temper
And headaches
But only my walls
Knew the cause
And the effect.
Through the years,
The empty walls
Of studio 251
The walls witnessed
My docility,
My passivity,
And my helplessness,
They also witnessed
My anger and whims,
My demands,
My disappointments
And self-defeats,
They frequently witnessed
My indifference
To some of my own
Achievements.

The empty walls
Witnessed
My episodes
Of depression
And mental weakness
But they also saw me
Put on a good face
Painting my lips
And faking strength.
The last day
When I moved out,
Studio 251
Looked cheerful,
Nice and bright,
Cozy and spacious
And full of possibilities.
And, as for me,
I slammed the door
Behind me
To start
A new phase of my life.

December 30, 1990

Goals

What do I want to be
When I grow up?
I want to be
A poet, a writer
And novelist
Where I leave
Pieces of me
And be an inspiration
To those who read.

Teaching
Is my last resort
But I am surrounded
With future teachers
In all my friends.
They drag me
To meetings, clubs,
Conferences, workshops
And field trips
Because
They enjoy my company.

I see they work
Towards their goals
And feed their dreams
Every day.
They learn and get trained
To educate
And entertain.
I pay attention
To their stories
To write about it later.

I confess,
I feel unaccomplished
With my dreams,
Often, I feel lost
To reach my goals
And wonder
What's the process
To be a successful
Writer
As they are in teaching?

May 30, 1984

The Lake

On foggy days,
Sunny, rainy,
Windy or cold,
We escaped
From the place
And the books
And drove down
To the lake
On Friday afternoons.
We enjoyed the view,
The company,
The picnics
And the friends.

Friends invite me
For a ride
Or, running errands,
We divert
From the road,
With no specific plan
We end up
At the lake.
We always
Find a good excuse
To get away
From the books
Or the school.

The beau suggests
An escape to the lake,
Just him and I,
But someone heard

And the group
Followed us.
I ride with him,
I want to talk
But the loud noise
From the engine
Doesn't let me hear.

The car doors'
Open and close
And our voices
And laughter
Fill the emptiness
And silence.
We disperse,
Off to the shoreline
Some go
And walk bare feet
By the water
That moves incessantly.
To the boardwalk
I go with my friend
And the beau
Comes behind me
Making efforts
To woo me.

We come together
And far from any
Disturbance
Or distractions,
It's nice to sit,
In the open air
And laugh and talk
Between my rivals
And all my friends.

Some girls
Fake innocence
But they don't fool
Anyone,
They walk,
Laugh and talk
So flirty
With the boys
And their hands
Are not contained,
They touch and brush
Wanting attention
But it's a joy to see
That the man
In our dispute
Has his eyes on me.

April 5, 1984

Technology

I was afraid
Of technology
And all devices
As I didn't want
To break anything.
While everyone used
The computers,
I used the typewriter
Or by hand I wrote,
While everyone
Used the modern stuff,
I was stubborn
In breaking my head
With rudimentary objects.
I was stubborn
In giving life and value
To what's not needed
Or no longer matters.

Well, I gave in
And I started
Using the computers.
I proved
Computers are fragile
And complicated
And my fear came true
When the computer
And the floppy disk
Ate my work
And my masterpieces.

Technology is amazing
When we let it
Simplify our work,
Things go smooth
And have a good ending
But it's confusing
With so many parts
And buttons,
Programs and spaces
Of information hidden
And every click
Can undo
What took all day long
To create.
Technology is fragile
And breaks so easily
If it announces,
'Floppy disk is corrupt,'
Even if I didn't touch
Or moved anything,
And technology
Is useless
If there's no electricity.

As much as I pray
Or get angry
And tap on it,
The computer doesn't
Spit back my work.
What happened?
I only used it yesterday
And everything
Was fine.
If it were on paper,
My problem and solution
Would be to look

In the trash can
For what I unwittingly
Threw away
And I'd start again.

Very disappointing
And annoying it is
To see my work
And my writing lost
Or there, in between,
May be hidden.
My works of art,
My homework
And my classes disappear
In a moment
And not even
The scientists
Know what to do
With this.

I barely start
Using the computer
And I realize,
Technology
Moves us forward
As it is faster
But holds us back
As, without the device
Or electricity,
Nothing gets done
And in a blackout
Or an oversight,
Everything is lost
And may never
Be recovered.

Technology
Makes us lazy,
Weak and dumb
And we get memory loss
Being dependent
On the machinery
That will replace us.

Technology
Is bad, evil
And vindictive
When it takes everything
Away from us
And from our hands
Because robots
Do everything
Better and faster,
Then we become
A hindrance in society
But are an instrument
For scientists.

Technology
Makes it easy
To get accustomed
To the good, easy,
Nice and fast things
Even if it is harmful
To human beings,
But returning
To the rudimentary,
It's self-sacrifice.

December 28, 1990

Blossoming

Like a delicate flower
Set in arid, hot,
Dry and infertile
Desert land,
So I was,
A withering flower
At the moment
For lack of humidity,
Wind, shade, and water.

I lacked a soft hand
And act of kindness,
Cognizant
Of my hidden beauty,
Who'd care for me
From the effects
Of the environment.
The delicate flower
Would then flourish
And the seed
Would spread
In new variants
To be resilient
And beautiful
In hard and dry regions.

Like a lost,
Lonely and scared girl,
Constantly with its back
Against the wall,
So I lived,
Cornering myself

For my sense
Of protection,
Always aware
Of the dangers
Of my surroundings,
Always protecting me
From rejection
And ill manners,
Always distrusting
And searching
For my safe corner
Even if the corner
Was in public
And out in the open.

I needed patience
And time,
I lacked words, care
And encouragement
To open my mental
And physical cage
To step outside
Assured and brave
And stop living
Hidden away.

Like a tiny thing
In a foreign world
Of giants
Where the steps
Resound,
Loud voices frighten,
Confuse and deafen,
So I felt,
Seeing me invisible,
Fragile, scared

And unable
To open my mouth
To ask for help
Or extend my hand
To help anyone else.

I lacked friends
Who'd walk with me
For me to feel protected,
Who'd share
Their light and strength
For me to be seen,
Friends to lift me up
Higher than them
So I'd see how great
It's always been.

Like a child
Among
Temperamental people,
So I lived,
Complacent
But silencing grievances,
Frustrations
And melancholy
And faking happiness
To make the impact
And time in place
More bearable.

I needed friends
Who'd let me speak
And vent
To get rid of beliefs
And preconceptions.
I needed strong role models

Who'd let me develop,
Emotionally
And socially,
And I needed
To meet friends
And mates,
But, frankly, I was scared.

In a few days,
With a smile
And short words,
Friends came to me,
And one by one,
Gave me their time,
Affection and respect.
The withering flower
Found relief
And began to thrive,
Conditioned and resilient
To the changes
In the environment.

What a difference
Friends make,
Because of them,
I see myself in the crowds,
I hear myself speak
Unafraid,
I hear myself give advice
And even commands
And I hear myself laugh
So carelessly
At my flaws
Because I feel good
Of who I am.

Now my smile
And good appearance
Are natural.
I no longer hide
From the mirrors
Or the people.
I feel good,
I feel important,
Appreciated and special.
I, quickly,
Stopped feeling
Like a lost girl
And I see myself
As an adult,
Strong and secure,
Now, I am
The flower bud
With the morning dew.

Because of my friends'
Flattery and inclusion,
I feel myself
Walking,
And breaking down
Obstacles
And I feel invincible.
My shyness disappeared,
The girl I was,
Became happy,
Assertive
And independent,
I am like a sprout
Always blossoming.

I have so many friends,
All of them
For different reasons
And in different ways,
But I feel loved
Even when I am alone.
There's always
Something to do,
There's always
Good company
And so much
To explore.
I love
Going to school
To see my friends,
I feel like a butterfly
In the spring fields
And always blossoming.

May 1, 1984

Cries

One winter night
With rain and winds,
Alone
And in the dark,
I listened
To the saddest
Caterwauling
That I had never heard.

It was a scary thing
That gave me
The chills,
It was a combination
Of sadness
And loneliness,
Hunger
And helplessness,
And it was something
Unrecognizable
And macabre,
It was noises
Of old voices
With the sound
Of a newborn
Crying aloud.

Where did it come from?
I don't know.
The screeching sounds,
Long, loud
And constant,
Broke my eardrums,

It penetrated my heart
And disturbed my mind.
It hurt me so much
What I heard
That I felt
As if my heart
Was being crushed,
It was such
An intense pain
That I burst into tears.

I had never heard
Things as such,
I had never felt
So much pain
From the noises outside
But this is
What happens
When cats
And their young,
Cry and meow
In the dark,
It leaves the ears
Of the naive
In bewilderment.

December 17, 1987

The Outdoors

Night falls upon us
And the conversation
Becomes dull
And repetitive
But it's still early,
According to my watch.

The cool of the night
Makes me shiver
But I feel the warmth
Of a blanket that smells
Like freshly washed
Fall upon my shoulders
Brings me comfort.
We gather around the fire
And hot cups of chocolate
Revives the chat.

The trees
Sway gently
But the breeze
Mixes in waves
Of cold air
That make me gasp.
I hear something
Hit the branches
High above
And my eyes get wide,
My hands hide,
My feet want to jump
At the table,
And my body tenses.

'Relax,
It's just a cat,'
Familiar voices say
And I hear concern
For my well-being
But my mind
Concentrates
On my phobias
That are powerful
And seem to be real.

I look at the ground,
Look at the black sky,
Look around
And shake the blanket,
I don't want bugs
Or any vermin
Near me.
That would be
A sure sudden death!
And I realize,
I need a repellent
Of every sort
To prevent
And drive away
All the animals
Of my nightmares.

I hear laughter
For what I do and say,
I hear comments
Belittling my feelings.
What can I do?
I am definitely
An indoor-person.

The tent
Gives the illusion
Of a safe refuge
But I close and cover
All the openings
And gaps
Just to be sure.
Laying down on the hard
And cold ground
And makes me achy
Impatient
And ill-tempered
Through my insomnia.

But, either way,
I wake up
With the aroma
Of hot fresh coffee
Brewing nearby.
I hear the sizzling
Of eggs and sausages
On the pan
And I rush to get out
And sit at the table.

There's nothing better
Than a hot cup of coffee
In my hands
And a good breakfast
On a chilly morning
To enjoy the outdoors,
Especially,
When the sun is up.

November 29, 1986

Carwash

We stood
On the sidewalk
With cardboard signs
Trying to attract
The drivers' attention.

The man
Of my interests
Crashed the event
But he comes ready
To mingle and help
As a good student
And friend.

I was the cashier,
My friends
Did the work
But I got paid.
It was a chilly day,
In early spring,
But no one
Complained.
Suds and water
Filled their hands
But they all talked
And laughed
Sharing the work
And what they had.
The music
In the background
From the radio nearby
And the water splashing

Filled the air
In those moments
When there was
Nothing to say.

The hours
Went by fast,
It always does
When I have fun
And others do the work.
It's a day off school
But all the girls
Look good
For the boys.
There is a bit
Of flirtatious looks
And sexy measured
Giggling
But the boys
Remain quiet
And unaware.

In the evening,
It was a surprise
To see the beau
At my door.
He brought me
My things
And showed
Some interest
In a conversation
With smiles
But no direct words.

This put an end
To the social battle
We had
And cemented
A new start.
I understood
That sometimes,
The interest is there
Even if we try
To deny it.
Sometimes,
We have to fight
Our own fears
And the bad tongues
To make us happy
And to have
Another chance.

March 30, 1984

Motherly Friend

I've been accused
Of being a motherly friend
But I take that
As a compliment.
How can I be a friend
And not say
Of what I see wrong?
How can I be a friend
And stand on the side
Watching the dangers
They step on
And not do anything?
How can I be a friend
And not rescue them
When they're in trouble?
How can I be a friend
And not give advice
Or sooth their pain?

November 25, 1983